DESIGN HEALTHY HAIR

“UNLOCK THE SECRETS TO HEALTHY HAIR WITH YOGA, MEDITATION, MORNING NATURE WALK, DIET AND MODERN SCIENCE AND TECHNOLOGY”

DR. SUNIL MISHRA

Made with ♥ on the Notion Press Platform
www.notionpress.com

Contents

Design Healthy Hair

SUBTITLE:

"Unlock the Secrets to Healthy Hair with Yoga, Meditation, Morning Nature Walk, Diet and Modern Science and Technology"

"Sleep well, Eat well and Breathe well to *Design Healthy Hair*"

Author: DR.SUNIL MISHRA

Acknowledgements

For
My parents, who teach me.
Dr. Rachita Dhurat, who guides me.
My wife and kids Dr Minal Mishra, Vedant and Adhyan, who inspire me.

Preface

It is with immense pride and joy that I write the preface for *Design Healthy Hair*, a work that represents both a culmination of cutting-edge science and the time-honored wisdom of holistic practices. Throughout my 35 years of experience in dermatology, with a particular focus on hair and hair disorders, I have witnessed the evolution of our understanding of hair health from superficial treatments to a more profound exploration of how our overall well-being directly influences the vitality of our hair.

When Dr. Sunil Mishra, the author of this book and someone I am proud to consider my student, shared his vision for Design Healthy Hair with me, I knew it was the result of years of hard work, dedication, and passion. His journey into the world of hair health is one I have had the honor of guiding, and watching him emerge as a respected figure in the field has been deeply fulfilling. His commitment to marrying ancient practices with modern scientific research is exactly what makes this book stand out. Dr. Mishra has skillfully crafted a comprehensive guide that reflects the true nature of hair health an expression of our overall physical, mental, and even gut health.

Design Healthy Hair is unique in the way it embraces both the traditional and the modern. Dr. Mishra takes readers on a journey through time-tested practices such as yoga, meditation, and a balanced diet, demonstrating how these approaches can transform not just the health of our hair, but our entire being. The inclusion of specific yoga asanas, Raj yoga meditation, and walking as integral aspects of cellular metabolism, disease prevention, and overall vitality highlights the role of holistic care in maintaining and improving hair health.

An aspect of this book that particularly excites me is the emphasis on the gut microbiome and its profound impact on hair health. This is an area of growing importance in both medical research and clinical practice. The gut, often referred to as the body's "second brain," plays a critical role in regulating not only our immune system but also our ability to absorb the nutrients essential for healthy hair growth. Dr. Mishra has adeptly explained how the delicate balance of microorganisms in the gut influences everything from inflammation to nutrient assimilation, showing how a healthy gut is vital for achieving and maintaining healthy hair. His insight into how life-force energy through diet nurtures this microbiome adds a fresh dimension to our understanding of hair wellness.

While Design Healthy Hair gives due credit to these ancient, holistic approaches, it is equally rooted in modern science. Dr. Mishra's exploration of current medical treatments such as cyclical nutritional therapy, DHT blockers, melatonin, and iPRF provides readers with a balanced and well-rounded understanding of the latest advancements in hair care. He seamlessly bridges the gap between natural remedies and scientific innovation, ensuring that readers have access to a broad spectrum of solutions for hair loss and hair care.

As someone who has had the privilege of teaching and mentoring dermatologists around the world, I can say with certainty that this book is poised to make a lasting impact. In Design Healthy Hair, Dr. Mishra has combined the practical with the profound, giving readers a blueprint for taking control of their hair health through informed lifestyle choices. His holistic approach goes beyond surface-level treatments and empowers readers to foster health from within.

I have known Dr. Sunil Mishra for many years, and his dedication to the field of hair care is exemplary. His journey from being my student to becoming a global educator in his own right has been a source of great pride for me. His meticulous research, personal experience, and unwavering commitment to excellence are evident on every page of this book. I am confident that Design Healthy Hair will not only inform but inspire readers to embrace a healthier, more mindful approach to their hair care.

In conclusion, I want to extend my deepest congratulations to Dr. Sunil Mishra for creating this remarkable guide. His insights into the interconnectedness of body, mind, and hair health will undoubtedly resonate with anyone seeking lasting solutions for healthier hair. Whether you are just beginning your journey toward better hair health or looking to refine your current regimen, this book offers the knowledge and guidance needed to make transformative changes.

Dr. Rachita Dhurat

Professor and Pioneer in Hair and Hair Disorder Treatments

Global Educator in Dermatology

Introduction

Introduction: The Path to Healthy Hair

Hair is more than just a physical attribute; it is often considered a symbol of vitality, health, and confidence. When a person experiences hair loss, it can be emotionally and psychologically challenging. As an experienced dermatologist with over 15 years of practice, I have encountered countless patients who struggle with hair loss. Many of them feel helpless, searching for quick fixes and miracle cures. However, the truth is that healthy hair is a reflection of a healthy body and mind. It is the result of a harmonious balance between our lifestyle choices, diet, mental well-being, and, when necessary, appropriate medical interventions.

This book, *Design Healthy Hair*, is intended to guide you on a holistic journey toward hair wellness. By addressing the root causes of hair loss and promoting a balanced, healthy lifestyle, you can achieve not only stronger, healthier hair but also improved overall well-being. This introduction will set the stage for the comprehensive approach we will explore together, emphasizing the interconnections between your physical health, mental peace, and hair vitality.

Understanding Hair Loss: Common Causes and Misconceptions

Hair loss is a multifaceted issue that can stem from a variety of causes. These can range from genetic predispositions, to Epigenetics like hormonal imbalances, and nutritional deficiencies to stress and environmental factors. Many people mistakenly believe that hair loss is solely an external problem that can be solved with topical treatments alone. While shampoos, serums, and other hair care products can play a supportive role, they are often not enough to address the underlying causes.

One of the most common misconceptions is that hair loss is an inevitable part of aging. While it's true that our hair changes as we age, losing large amounts of hair is not something you simply have to accept. By understanding the causes and contributing factors of hair loss, you can take proactive steps to mitigate its impact and, in many cases, reverse it.

The Holistic Approach to Hair Health: Mind, Body, and Spirit

The foundation of this book is the belief that hair health cannot be separated from overall health. A truly effective approach to combating hair loss and promoting hair growth must involve a comprehensive lifestyle transformation. This involves integrating practices that nurture not just your body, but also your mind and spirit.

1. The Mind-Body Connection: Stress is a major contributor to hair loss. Chronic stress can lead to a condition known as Telogen effluvium, where hair prematurely enters the resting phase and falls out more easily. It can also exacerbate conditions like Alopecia areata, where the immune system attacks hair follicles. Therefore, managing stress through techniques like meditation and yoga is crucial for maintaining healthy hair.

Meditation, particularly Raj Yoga meditation, plays a significant role in this process. Raj Yoga is a form of meditation that focuses on attaining a deep state of relaxation and inner peace. By practicing this meditation regularly, you can reduce the physical and psychological effects of stress, promoting a healthy scalp environment conducive to hair growth.

2. The Power of Physical Activity: Regular exercise, such as a 45-minute early morning walk, is another key component of a healthy lifestyle that supports hair health. Walking not only improves circulation, ensuring that your hair follicles receive a steady supply of nutrients and oxygen, but it also boosts overall metabolism. This increased metabolic activity can lead to better hormonal balance and improved digestion, both of which are essential for healthy hair.

Additionally, specific yoga asanas, or postures, can further enhance blood flow to the scalp, support hormonal regulation, and reduce stress. In this book, you'll learn about the most effective yoga poses for promoting hair growth and how to incorporate them into your daily routine.

3. Nourishing Your Body from Within: Your diet plays a critical role in the health of your hair. Just as plants need the right nutrients to grow, so do your hair follicles. A diet rich in vitamins, minerals, and life force energy an ancient concept referring to the vital energy present in natural, whole foods can significantly impact hair health.

In the chapters that follow, we will explore how the foods you eat affect your gut microbiome, which in turn influences your hair. A balanced, nutrient-rich diet supports the growth of healthy bacteria in your gut, which is essential for optimal nutrient absorption and, consequently, for nourishing your hair from within.

4. Modern Medical Interventions: While lifestyle changes are fundamental to improving hair health, modern medical treatments also have their place. Advances in dermatology have provided us with a range of effective treatments for hair loss, from DHT blockers to Minoxidil and Melatonin supplements to innovative procedures like iPRF (Injectable Platelet-Rich Fibrin) therapy. These treatments can complement your holistic approach, offering additional support where need.

In this book, we will discuss how these treatments work, who can benefit from them, and how they can be integrated into your overall hair health plan. It is important to approach hair loss treatment with a well-rounded strategy, combining the best of both traditional practices and modern science.

A Journey, Not a Destination

As you begin this journey toward healthier hair, it's important to recognize that there are no overnight miracles. Hair growth is a gradual process, and the changes you make today will take time to show results. However, by committing to a balanced lifestyle that supports your mind, body, and spirit, you can create the optimal conditions for your hair to thrive.

This book is designed to be your companion on this journey, providing you with practical advice, scientific insights, and motivational guidance. Whether you are just beginning to notice thinning hair or have been struggling with hair loss for years, the strategies outlined in *Design Healthy Hair* will empower you to take control of your hair health. Sleep well, eat well and breathe well to design your healthy hair.

Remember, healthy hair is a reflection of a healthy you. By embracing the holistic approach detailed in this book, you are not just addressing the symptoms of hair loss; you are fostering a deeper sense of well-being that will benefit every aspect of your life. Let's embark on this journey together, with the understanding that true beauty and vitality come from within.

This introduction sets the tone for the rest of the book, emphasizing the interconnectedness of physical health, mental well-being, and hair vitality. It encourages readers to approach hair health as a journey, one that requires patience, commitment, and a holistic perspective. The content of this book is somewhat midway between a story book novel and a medical journal. So, it is essential to consult an expert before embarking on the journey of designing healthy hair.

CHAPTER ONE

The Science of Hair Growth

Hair is one of the most defining features of our appearance, yet its biology is complex and often misunderstood. To understand how to promote healthy hair growth and combat hair loss, it's essential to grasp the fundamental science behind hair growth. This chapter will delve into the intricacies of the hair growth cycle, the factors that influence it, and the latest research on maintaining healthy hair.

1.1 **The Hair Growth Cycle: An Overview**

Hair growth is a cyclical process that involves several phases. Each hair follicle on your scalp goes through this cycle independently of others, which is why hair loss typically appears gradual rather than sudden. The three main phases of the hair growth cycle are:

1. Anagen Phase (Growth Phase):

The anagen phase is the active growth period of the hair follicle, lasting anywhere from 2 to 7 years, depending on genetics and other factors. During this phase, hair cells in the root of the hair follicle divide rapidly, adding to the hair shaft and making the hair grow longer.

The length of the anagen phase determines how long hair can grow before it stops. For example, people with a longer anagen phase can grow their hair longer than those with a shorter phase.

2. **Catagen Phase (Transition Phase):**

The catagen phase is a brief period, typically lasting around 2 to 3 weeks, during which the hair follicle transitions from active growth to a resting state. In this phase, the hair follicle shrinks, and the lower part of the follicle is destroyed. The hair strand, now called a club hair, is cut off from the blood supply and from the cells that produce new hair.

The catagen phase signals the end of active hair growth and prepares the follicle for the next stage.

3. **Telogen Phase (Resting Phase):**

The telogen phase lasts around 3 to 4 months and is the resting period of the hair follicle. During this phase, the hair does not grow but remains in the follicle. About 10-15% of all hairs are in this phase at any given time.

At the end of the telogen phase, the hair follicle re-enters the anagen phase, and the existing club hair is shed to make room for a new hair strand.

4. **Exogen Phase (Shedding Phase):**

Some researchers include a fourth phase called the exogen phase, during which the hair is shed from the scalp. This phase is considered a continuation of the telogen phase. It's normal to shed 50-100 hairs daily as part of the natural hair growth cycle.

Understanding these phases is crucial because disruptions in any of these stages can lead to hair loss. For example, if too many hairs enter the telogen phase prematurely, a condition known as telogen effluvium can occur, leading to noticeable thinning.

1.2 Factors Influencing Hair Growth

Genetics:

Genetics play an important role in the length, density, and overall health of your hair. Genetics, either paternal or maternal is directly associated with various types of hair loss, like Androgenetic alopecia, Alopecia areata or Cicatricial alopecia. When only one parent (maternal of paternal) genetic is involved, the hair loss is relatively milder whereas when both parent genetics are involved, the hair loss starts at an early stage as well as rapid and severe in nature. This is the reason why many patients of hair loss blame their parents for their hair loss. However, this is not completely true. A better scientific understanding is required rather than just listening to social media and bloggers.

Epigenetics:

While genetics play a significant role in hair loss and hair thinning, other aspects of our day-to-day routine which are called epigenetics, such as lifestyle, stress, hormones, nutrition, pollution, infection and cosmetics also have a greater impact. Epigenetics are external factors of our life which may modify the expression of our inner genetics. Hair loss Gene is like a seed inside the soil, it will grow into a plant (hair loss) only when you provide fertilizer and water of bad Epigenetics. A person with strong genetic predisposition to hair loss can prevent hair loss and maintain good hair by improvising his Epigenetics. So, in today's era Epigenetic are more contributory for causing diseases and hair loss rather than just genetics.

As a result, understanding epigenetic and learning to correct them is the need of time. The easiest and the most cost effect method to improvise the epigenetic is by sleeping early, getting up early morning and performing the morning ritual of yoga, meditation and nature walk for 45 mins. Intake of good balanced nutritive diet with life force energy on time during the day. We will be covering these aspects in details in the following chapters.

1.2.1 Hormones and Hair Growth

Androgens: Androgens are male hormones like testosterone and dihydrotestosterone (DHT), which can influence hair growth patterns. While androgens are essential for normal hair growth in certain body areas, they can have the opposite effect on the scalp.

DHT, a derivative of testosterone, is also a stress hormone, known to shrink hair follicles (miniaturization) in genetically predisposed individuals, leading to androgenetic alopecia, commonly known as male or female pattern baldness. This condition is the most common cause of hair loss, affecting both men and women. Late sleep, stressful life and wrong selection of diet influence and increase the activity of DHT on hair follicle.

Estrogen: Estrogen, a female hormone, plays a protective role in hair growth. Higher levels of estrogen are associated with prolonged anagen phases, which is why many women experience thicker, more lustrous hair during pregnancy. However, after childbirth, when estrogen levels drop, many women experience a form of hair loss known as postpartum telogen effluvium. It occurs very commonly after 3 to 6 months after delivery.

Thyroid Hormones: The thyroid gland regulates metabolism, and its hormones, thyroxine (T4) and triiodothyronine (T3), significantly affect hair growth. Both hyperthyroidism (overactive thyroid) and hypothyroidism (underactive thyroid) can lead to hair thinning and loss. Ensuring thyroid hormone levels are balanced is crucial for maintaining healthy hair.

1.2.2 Nutrition and Hair Growth

Proteins: Hair is primarily composed of a protein called keratin. Adequate protein intake is essential for hair growth since it provides the building blocks (amino acids) that hair follicles need to produce new hair. A deficiency in protein can lead to weak, brittle hair or even hair loss.

Vitamins and Minerals: Several vitamins and minerals are critical for hair health: the list is long, but we will cover few important ones here.

Biotin (Vitamin B7): Essential for keratin production, biotin deficiency can lead to hair thinning and hair loss. Many hair growth supplements contain biotin due to its beneficial effects on hair strength and growth.

Iron: Iron deficiency is a common cause of hair loss, particularly in women. Iron is vital for producing hemoglobin, which carries oxygen to hair follicles, promoting healthy hair growth.**Calcium** & **Vitamin D:** Vitamin D plays a role in hair follicle cycling, and its deficiency is linked to hair loss conditions like alopecia areata.

Zinc: Zinc is important for hair tissue growth and repair. A deficiency can lead to hair loss and scalp issues.

Copper: Copper aids in the production of melanin, which maintains hair color and prevents premature graying, while also supporting healthy hair follicles.

Vitamin C: Essential for collagen production, Vitamin C strengthens hair strands and helps with iron absorption, which is vital for hair growth.

Vitamin A: Vital for the production of sebum, Vitamin A keeps the scalp moisturized, promoting healthy hair growth and preventing dry, brittle hair.

Vitamin E: Known for its antioxidant properties, Vitamin E improves blood circulation in the scalp, supports hair follicle health, and adds shine to the hair.

Vitamin B12: Important for red blood cell production, Vitamin B12 ensures that hair follicles receive enough oxygen, supporting healthy hair growth.

Magnesium: Magnesium reduces inflammation and helps balance calcium levels, preventing hair follicle calcification, which can lead to hair thinning.

Vitamin B6: This vitamin supports protein metabolism and helps produce red blood cells, both crucial for nourishing hair follicles and promoting healthy hair growth.

Folic Acid: Folic acid supports the formation of healthy red blood cells and promotes the growth of new hair cells, making it essential for hair regeneration and preventing thinning.

Omega-3 Fatty Acids: Omega-3s are essential fats that your body cannot make but must be obtained from your diet. These fatty acids have anti-inflammatory properties, which can help open hair follicles and promote healthy hair growth. Foods rich in omega-3s include fatty fish, walnuts, and flaxseeds.

Here I would like to discuss few very important aspects of nutritional value of our food. Almost all my patients believe and say that they were eating healthy and nutritive diet in adequate amount and still facing hair loss and hair thinning. But the important question is, whether our food actually is containing adequate amount of nutrition as we believe. I started exploring more about this and then understood that the issue starts from the farming technique of modern farming. Our ancestors used to use manure and compost for traditional farming. This technique had less phosphorous content in the soil and more of minerals like copper, magnesium, calcium, iron, and zinc. Hence the nutritive value of the crops was actually higher.

Modern day farming involves usage of fertilizers and pesticides which has higher phosphorous content. The high phosphorus content kills the good and friendly bacteria and mycorrhiza fungus in the soil. Mycorrhiza fungus has a symbiotic relationship with plant roots. They perform the barter system wherein they take the sugars made by plants and give it to the soil Bacteria and in return take minerals from the bacteria and give to the plant in exchange. This exchange is lost when the fungus and bacteria are killed by fertilizers and pesticides. As a result, the sugar content of the plant remains within it, resulting in increase of the size and bulk of crop without increase in the mineral content. So, the nutritive value of the crop i.e copper, calcium, magnesium, vitamin C, riboflavin fall drastically (30 to 50%) but the size of the crop increases.

Now when you consume such food, the nutritive value is less at the origin itself. This causes few adverse effects on the body health in form of auto immune diseases, nutritive hunger, subclinical deficiencies and compensatory failure. We are a society today which is over fed yet malnourished in terms of nutritional assets. This is also a crucial aspect of hair loss in today's generation. We will read more about this aspect in following chapters.

1.2.3 Stress and Hair Growth

Stress is one of the most important Epigenetic in today's era which causes hair loss and hair thinning. But it's often neglected aspect as we are not aware of its existence. We all need to really understand what is stress. We all may have work pressure, financial pressure, studies pressure etc., but does that mean its stress. Stress is actually the outcome of how you respond to these external pressures by your coping ability of life.

Stress = External Pressure / Coping Ability

External pressure may be multiple in life and is mostly not in our control. Your boss shouted at you, your mom did not give you money, your shares fell in stock market. But the coping ability, which is totally in your control, is how you respond to this external pressure. It's very important to increase the coping ability in your life by meditation and uplifting your subconscious.

E.g.: If someone throws a cockroach on a girl, she might start jumping and shouting (Stress)

Whereas if a cockroach is thrown on a stable meditative mind person, he or she will just remove the cockroach from his or her body and continue his life (non-stress). We will learn more about increasing the coping ability in later chapters.

Physical Stress: Physical stressors such as surgery, illness, or drastic weight loss can shock the hair growth cycle, pushing more hairs into the telogen phase, leading to increased shedding. This type of hair loss, called telogen effluvium, is usually temporary but can be distressing.

Emotional Stress: Emotional stress is also a significant factor in hair loss. Chronic stress can lead to conditions like telogen effluvium and even trigger autoimmune conditions like alopecia areata, where the immune system attacks hair follicles, causing patches of hair to fall out.

1.2.3 Environmental Factors

Infection: Infections on the scalp can damage hair follicles and disrupt the hair growth cycle. Fungal infections like ringworm (tinea capitis) can cause patches of hair loss, while bacterial infections can lead to folliculitis, an inflammation of hair follicles that weakens hair strands. In some cases, infections trigger an immune response that leads to excessive shedding or scarring alopecia, where hair loss may become permanent if not treated promptly. Treating scalp infections with antifungal or antibacterial agents is crucial to restore healthy hair growth.

Sun Exposure: Prolonged exposure to the sun's ultraviolet (UV) rays can damage hair and scalp. UV rays break down the hair's protein structure, leading to weakened strands and split ends. The scalp can also get sunburned, which may affect hair growth.

Pollution: Environmental pollutants, including dust, smoke, and airborne toxins, can settle on the scalp and hair, causing oxidative stress and damage to hair follicles. Over time, this can lead to weakened hair and hair loss.

Cosmetics and Chemical Exposure: Frequent use of harsh hair treatments, such as coloring, perming, or chemical straightening, can damage the hair shaft and weaken the follicles. Overuse of these treatments can lead to hair breakage and loss.

1.3 Research Insights on Hair Growth

Recent research has provided valuable insights into the complex biology of hair growth, leading to innovative treatments and a deeper understanding of how to maintain healthy hair.

1.3.1 Stem Cell Research

Stem cells play a critical role in hair growth and regeneration. Hair follicles contain a small population of stem cells located in the bulge area of the follicle. These stem cells are activated during the anagen phase to regenerate the hair follicle and produce new hair.

Research is ongoing to harness stem cells for hair regeneration. Techniques like platelet-rich plasma (PRP) and injectable platelet-rich fibrin (iPRF) aim to stimulate these stem cells, encouraging hair regrowth in areas affected by thinning or baldness.

1.3.2 The Role of Microbiome in Hair Growth

The gut microbiome the collection of bacteria, viruses, and other microorganisms living in your intestineshas been found to influence hair health. A balanced gut microbiome is essential for proper nutrient absorption, which directly impacts hair growth.
Recent studies suggest that an unhealthy gut microbiome may contribute to hair loss conditions like Alopecia areata and Androgenetic alopecia. Probiotics and a diet rich in fiber, fermented foods, and prebiotics can help maintain a healthy gut, promoting better hair growth.

1.3.3 Advances in Hair Loss Treatments

Cyclical Nutritional Therapy:

As we have read and understood about the nutritional deficiency in our food from farms, it becomes important to compensate for the deficiency by taking some supplements. This approach involves taking low dose specific vitamins, minerals, and supplements in a cyclical manner to prevent nutrient imbalances and promote hair growth.

Also, another aspect is that some nutritional elements are friends of each other, so it's advisable to take them together to help in absorption and metabolism (eg Iron if taken along with vitamin C and vitamin A helps in absorption and metabolism). On the other hand, there are some nutritional elements which are not so good friends of each other. So, it's advisable to not take them together, eg (Iron and Calcium if taken together inhibits their absorption and utilization).

Having said that there are studies which shows that nutrients if taken on consecutive days give better results than taking it every day. Iron supplement if taken alternate days gives better absorption and utilization by

body rather than daily intake.
Also, it is based on the understanding that different nutrients are needed at different times during the hair growth cycle.

DHT Inhibitors: Research continues to explore new ways to inhibit DHT, the hormone responsible for Androgenetic alopecia. Medications like finasteride, dutasteride and topical treatments containing saw palmetto, coconut oil or pumpkin seed oil are examples of DHT inhibitors currently used to treat hair loss.

Minoxidil: This molecule has been applied on the scalp since few decades for hair regrowth. It works by increasing the blood flow to hair on the scalp and helps in delivery of oxygen and nutrition to the hair bulb and the stem cell area. Now there are tablets forms of minoxidil which gives better results in terms of increasing hair thickness and density when taken in low doses.

1.4 The Path Forward: A Holistic Approach to Hair Health

While understanding the science of hair growth is crucial, it's equally important to take a holistic approach to hair care. By addressing not just the symptoms of hair loss but also the underlying causes, you can create an environment where your hair can thrive.

In the chapters that follow, we'll explore practical strategies for improving your hair health, from optimizing your diet with better life force energy and managing stress by increasing the coping ability to incorporating yoga and meditation into your daily routine. We'll also discuss how to integrate modern treatments with these lifestyle changes to achieve the best possible outcomes for your hair.

Remember, healthy hair is a reflection of a healthy body and mind. By understanding the science behind hair growth and taking a comprehensive approach to your hair care routine, you can promote not only stronger, healthier hair but also an overall sense of well-being.

CHAPTER TWO

THE ROLE OF THE NUTRITION AND GUT MICROBIOME IN HAIR HEALTH

In recent years, scientific research has increasingly highlighted the critical role the gut microbiome plays in overall health, including skin and hair health. While this connection may not seem obvious at first, the gut is integral to various bodily functions, from nutrient absorption to immune system regulation. Understanding the relationship between the gut microbiome and hair growth can provide new insights into maintaining healthy hair and addressing hair loss. This chapter delves into the gut-hair connection, exploring how a balanced microbiome supports hair growth and what you can do to optimize your gut health for better hair.

2.1 Understanding the Gut Microbiome

The gut microbiome refers to the trillions of microorganisms including bacteria, viruses, fungi, and other microbes that reside in your digestive tract. These microorganisms are not just passive inhabitants; they play an active role in various physiological processes, many of which are crucial for overall health. These microorganisms are our friends in our gut. They help in maintaining our mental health, physical health at cellular level and our hair health. These organisms survive on the fibres (mostly plant based) which we eat in our diet. That is the reason why we need to eat more of plant based fibrous food which doesn't get digested and absorbed before entering the gut. If our diet is missing with theses fibers, the friendly microorganisms either start dying or they start eating away the mucin (a protective membrane lining of our intestine wall), thereby creating holes in the membrane. This causes 'leaky gut' and many harmful proteins and bacteria in our food can easily enter the gut wall and then blood. This gives arise to many auto immune contain like Alopecia areata, Cicatricial alopecia, joint pains, allergies etc. It is so important to feed our friendly microorganisms and maintain the gut microbiome to avoid many diseases and maintain an overall health. It is no wonder that the Gut is called the "Second Brain" now. One of the easiest methods to maintain healthy gut microbiome is to eat homemade well-cooked food with high life force energy and to avoid outside restaurant food.

2.1.1 The Composition of the Gut Microbiome

The human gut microbiome is incredibly diverse, with hundreds of different species of bacteria and other microorganisms. The composition of your gut microbiome is unique to you, influenced by factors such as diet, lifestyle, genetics, and even your environment.

The most well-known bacterial phyla in the gut are Firmicutes and Bacteroidetes, but other groups such as Actinobacteria and Proteobacteria also play important roles. The balance among these microbial populations is crucial for maintaining gut health.

2.1.2 Functions of the Gut Microbiome

Digestion and Nutrient Absorption: The gut microbiome helps break down food, particularly complex carbohydrates and fibers that are otherwise indigestible. By doing so, it aids in the absorption of essential nutrients like vitamins, minerals, and amino acids that are critical for hair growth.

Immune System Regulation: Approximately 70% of the immune system is housed in the gut. The gut microbiome plays a key role in regulating immune responses, protecting against pathogens, and reducing inflammation. Chronic inflammation, often linked to an imbalanced gut microbiome, can negatively impact hair growth.

Hormonal Balance: The gut microbiome also influences hormone production and regulation, including hormones like estrogen and cortisol, which can affect hair growth. For example, an overgrowth of certain gut bacteria can increase the production of androgens, which are linked to hair loss.

2.2 The Gut-Hair Connection: How Your Gut Affects Your Hair

Healthy hair growth depends on a complex interplay of factors, including the nutrients available to hair follicles, the immune environment surrounding the follicles, and the hormonal signals they receive. The gut microbiome influences all these factors, making it a critical determinant of hair health.

2.2.1 Nutrient Absorption and Hair Growth

Vitamins and Minerals: The gut microbiome assists in the production and absorption of several vitamins and minerals essential for hair growth which we had enlisted in the previous chapter 1, have listed here again for the convenience. For example:
Biotin: Some gut bacteria synthesize biotin, a B vitamin that strengthens hair and promotes growth.
Iron: A healthy gut is necessary for the proper absorption of iron. Iron deficiency is a common cause of hair loss, particularly in women.
Calcium &Vitamin D: The gut microbiome helps metabolize vitamin D, which plays a role in hair follicle cycling.
Zinc: Zinc is important for hair tissue growth and repair. A deficiency can lead to hair loss and scalp issues.
Copper: Copper aids in the production of melanin, which maintains hair color and prevents premature graying, while also supporting healthy hair follicles.
Vitamin C: Essential for collagen production, Vitamin C strengthens hair strands and helps with iron absorption, which is vital for hair growth.
Vitamin A: Vital for the production of sebum, Vitamin A keeps the scalp moisturized, promoting healthy hair growth and preventing dry, brittle hair.
Vitamin E: Known for its antioxidant properties, Vitamin E improves blood circulation in the scalp, supports hair follicle health, and adds shine to the hair.

Vitamin B12: Important for red blood cell production, Vitamin B12 ensures that hair follicles receive enough oxygen, supporting healthy hair growth.
Magnesium: Magnesium reduces inflammation and helps balance calcium levels, preventing hair follicle calcification, which can lead to hair thinning.
Vitamin B6: This vitamin supports protein metabolism and helps produce red blood cells, both crucial for nourishing hair follicles and promoting healthy hair growth.
Folic Acid: Folic acid supports the formation of healthy red blood cells and promotes the growth of new hair cells, making it essential for hair regeneration and preventing thinning.
Amino Acids: Protein digestion and the absorption of amino acids, the building blocks of hair keratin, depend on a well-functioning gut. An imbalance in the gut microbiome can lead to malabsorption of these crucial nutrients, resulting in weaker hair or increased hair loss.

2.2.2 Immune System and Inflammation

Chronic Inflammation: An imbalanced gut microbiome can lead to a condition known as "leaky gut," where the intestinal lining becomes more permeable (transfer of particles from intestine to blood). As we had discussed earlier that a diet less in plan-based fibre causes the friendly gut microorganisms to either die or they start eating the protective mucin layer. This causes minor holes in the membranes and increases the permeability. This permeability then allows toxins and partially digested food particles to enter the bloodstream, our immune system gets alarmed and starts producing more immune cells and cytokines, triggering systemic inflammation. Chronic inflammation can affect the scalp and hair follicles, potentially leading to conditions like Alopecia areata, Telogen effluvium, Androgenetic alopecia or even Cicatricial alopecia.

Autoimmune Conditions: Research suggests that the gut microbiome plays a role in the development of autoimmune conditions also. The pathway is the same like chronic inflammation which we discussed in above paragraph, but here the immune cells gets misguided and start attacking our own cells and tissues like hair follicles. This cross reactivity is called Auto-immune condition. Conditions like Alopecia areata, where the immune system targets hair follicles, have been linked to imbalances in the gut microbiome. We have seen many cases of Alopecia areata in children due to wrong food in their diet. Especially the junk, processed and packed food. By correcting the diet of children, providing cyclical nutritional supplement and minimal medications we can control and treat the gut microbiome, correct the "leaky gut" and then the alopecia areata effectively.

2.2.3 Hormonal Regulation

Cortisol and Stress: The gut microbiome can influence the body's stress response by regulating the production of cortisol, the primary stress hormone. Chronic stress and elevated cortisol levels can disrupt the hair growth cycle, leading to increased hair shedding. By maintaining a healthy gut, you can help manage stress and support hormonal balance, promoting healthier hair growth.

Estrogen Metabolism: Gut bacteria play a role in the metabolism of estrogen. An imbalance in the gut microbiome can disrupt this process, potentially leading to estrogen dominance, which has been linked to hair thinning, particularly in women.

2.3 Research on the Gut Microbiome and Hair Health

Recent studies have begun to uncover the specific ways in which the gut microbiome influences hair growth and health. While this area of research is still emerging, the findings thus far highlight the potential for targeting the gut microbiome as part of a holistic approach to hair care.

2.3.1 Studies on Gut Health and Hair Loss

Alopecia areata: A study published in *Nature* found that individuals with Alopecia areata had distinct differences in their gut microbiome compared to those without the condition. The research suggested that targeting the gut microbiome with specific probiotics or dietary changes could potentially improve outcomes for people with this autoimmune form of hair loss.

Pattern Baldness: Another study conducted by Japanese researchers found a correlation between the composition of the gut microbiome and Androgenetic alopecia (male and female pattern baldness). The researchers noted that certain bacterial profiles were more prevalent in individuals with this form of hair loss, indicating that the gut microbiome might influence susceptibility to Androgenetic alopecia.

2.3.2 Probiotics and Hair Growth

Probiotic Supplementation: Probiotics, which are beneficial bacteria that support gut health, have been studied for their potential to improve hair growth. For example, a study published in *Experimental Dermatology* found that mice supplemented with the probiotic *Lactobacillus reuteri* showed significant improvements in hair growth and density, attributed to reduced systemic inflammation and improved skin barrier function.

Human Trials: Although more research is needed, early human trials suggest that certain probiotics may help manage hair loss by improving gut health and reducing inflammation. Probiotic-rich foods like yogurt, kefir, butter milk, sauerkraut, and kimchi could potentially benefit hair health by supporting a balanced gut microbiome.

2.3.3 The Role of Prebiotics

Feeding the Microbiome: Prebiotics are non-digestible fibers that feed the beneficial bacteria in your gut. By promoting the growth of these good bacteria, prebiotics help maintain a healthy gut environment. Foods rich in prebiotics, such as garlic, onions, bananas, and asparagus, can support hair health indirectly by fostering a thriving gut microbiome.

2.4 How to Optimize Gut Health for Better Hair

Maintaining a healthy gut microbiome is essential for supporting hair growth and preventing hair loss. Here are some practical steps you can take to optimize your gut health:

2.4.1 Dietary Strategies

Eat a Diverse Diet: A diverse diet rich in different types of fruits, vegetables, whole grains, and lean proteins can help promote a diverse gut microbiome, which is associated with better overall health, including hair health.

Include Probiotic Foods: Regularly consuming probiotic-rich foods like yogurt, kefir, butter milk, sauerkraut, kimchi, miso, and tempeh can help populate your gut with beneficial bacteria. These foods support a balanced microbiome, which is crucial for nutrient absorption and immune regulation.

Increase Prebiotic Intake: Incorporating prebiotic-rich foods like garlic, onions, leeks, asparagus, bananas, and oats into your diet can help nourish the beneficial bacteria in your gut, supporting a healthy microbiome.

2.4.2 Lifestyle Changes

Manage Stress: Chronic stress can disrupt the gut microbiome, leading to dysbiosis (an imbalance of gut bacteria) and increased inflammation. Practices like yoga, meditation, and deep breathing can help manage stress levels and support a healthy gut.

Exercise Regularly: Regular physical activity has been shown to positively influence the gut microbiome, promoting the growth of beneficial bacteria. Exercise also supports healthy digestion and reduces inflammation, both of which are important for hair health.

Avoid Antibiotics When Possible: While antibiotics are sometimes necessary, they can disrupt the gut microbiome by killing off beneficial bacteria. If you need to take antibiotics, consider supplementing with probiotics during and after your course of treatment to help restore your gut microbiome.

2.4.3 Supplements for Gut and Hair Health

Probiotic Supplements: If you have specific gut health concerns or are unable to get enough probiotics from your diet, consider taking a high-quality probiotic supplement. Look for a product that contains multiple strains of bacteria and has a high CFU (colony-forming units) count.

Digestive Enzymes: For individuals with digestive issues that affect nutrient absorption, digestive enzyme supplements can help break down food more effectively, ensuring that your body and your hair gets the nutrients it needs.

Omega-3 Fatty Acids: Omega-3 supplements, such as fish oil, can help reduce inflammation and support a healthy gut microbiome. These fatty acids also play a role in maintaining the health of hair follicles.

Fecal microbiome transplant (FMT): It is an emerging treatment that involves transferring healthy gut bacteria from a donor person to a recipient person to restore balance of the gut microbiome. FMT has gained attention for its potential role in improving overall health, including hair growth. A healthy gut microbiome is crucial for optimal nutrient absorption and hormonal balance, both of which are essential for healthy hair. Disruptions in gut health can lead to inflammation, auto immune condition and stress, which may trigger hair loss. Recent studies suggest that restoring gut microbiota through FMT can improve digestive health, reduce inflammation, reduce auto immune cells and cytokines and potentially support hair growth by enhancing the body's ability to absorb nutrients vital for hair, such as biotin, zinc, and vitamins D and E. It has been tried in severe Alopecia areata, Telogen effluvium and Androgenetic alopecia patients with good success rate. While research is still evolving, FMT offers a promising future for holistic approaches to hair care by addressing underlying gut imbalances that may contribute to hair thinning or loss.

2.5 Real-Life Applications: Case Studies and Practical Tips

Understanding the connection between gut health and hair growth is just the first step. Applying this knowledge to your daily life can make a significant difference in the health and appearance of your hair. In this section, we'll explore real-life case studies and provide practical tips for optimizing gut health to support better hair growth.

2.5.1 Case Study: Reversing Telogen effluvium through Gut Health

A 35-year-old woman experienced significant hair thinning after a period of intense stress. She also reported digestive issues, including bloating and irregular bowel movements. Upon evaluating her diet and lifestyle, it was clear that her gut health was compromised, likely contributing to her hair loss.

After implementing a gut health-focused approach - including a probiotic supplement, increased intake of prebiotic foods, and regular yoga practice - her digestive issues improved, and her hair began to regrow. Within six months, she reported significant improvement in both her hair thickness and overall well-being.

2.5.2 Practical Tips for Daily Gut Care

Start Your Day with Fiber: Begin your day with a fiber-rich breakfast, such as oatmeal topped with fruits and nuts. Fiber supports a healthy gut by feeding beneficial bacteria.

Incorporate Fermented Foods: Add a serving of fermented foods to at least one meal each day. For example, include butter milk, kimchi or sauerkraut in your lunch or enjoy a serving of yogurt as a snack.

Stay Hydrated: Drinking plenty of water is essential for digestion and helps maintain a healthy gut environment. Aim for at least eight glasses of water per day.

2.6 The Future of Gut Health and Hair Care

As research on the gut microbiome continues to evolve, new insights into the connection between gut health and hair growth are likely to emerge. The potential for personalized probiotic therapies and dietary interventions tailored to individual gut microbiomes offers exciting possibilities for the future of hair care.

2.6.1 Personalized Probiotics

Advances in genetic testing and microbiome analysis may soon allow for the development of personalized probiotics tailored to an individual's unique gut microbiome. These targeted therapies could address specific imbalances that contribute to hair loss, offering a new frontier in hair care.

2.6.2 Gut-Brain-Hair Axis

Emerging research is also exploring the gut-brain-hair axis, a concept that links gut health, mental health, and hair health. Understanding this connection could lead to holistic treatment approaches that address the root causes of hair loss, particularly in stress-related conditions like Telogen effluvium and Alopecia areata.

Conclusion

The gut microbiome plays a crucial role in hair health, influencing everything from nutrient absorption to immune function, auto immune condition and hormonal balance. By prioritizing gut health through diet, lifestyle changes, and potentially cyclical nutritional supplements, you can create a strong foundation for healthy hair growth. As research continues to uncover new links between the gut and hair, embracing a gut-focused approach to hair care could be one of the most effective strategies for maintaining and restoring healthy hair.

In the next chapter, we will explore how life force energy and diet directly impact your hair, providing practical dietary guidelines to nourish your body and your hair from the inside out.

CHAPTER THREE

LIFE FORCE ENERGY AND DIET

When it comes to hair health, the food you consume plays a fundamental role. But it's not just about counting calories or macronutrients; it's about understanding the life force energy in the food you eat and how it influences your body at a cellular level. Food cooked by yourself or your mom (vibration of love and affection) with fresh raw materials in your house will have higher life force energy as compared to the same food cooked by a chef (vibration of money and stress) with deep freeze raw materials in a restaurant. Both the food may have the same calories and macronutrients in it, yet its way different in aspect of life force energy. This chapter explores the concept of life force energy, how it connects to ancient practices and modern science, and how to harness this energy through diet to promote healthy hair.

3.1 Understanding Life Force Energy

The concept of life force energy, often referred to as "Prana" in Indian philosophy, "Qi" in Chinese medicine, or "Vital Force" in other traditions, is an ancient idea that posits an essential energy flowing through all living things. This energy is believed to be the source of vitality, health, and well-being. In the context of hair health, life force energy is the dynamic force that sustains the cells, tissues, and processes that contribute to hair growth.

3.1.1 Ancient Wisdom Meets Modern Science

Prana and Ayurvedic Traditions: In Ayurveda, Prana is considered the vital life force that is present in all living beings and is particularly concentrated in fresh, whole foods. Foods that are rich in Prana are thought to support health, vitality, and longevity, including the health of your hair.

Qi in Traditional Chinese Medicine (TCM): Similarly, in TCM, Qi is the vital energy that flows through the body's meridians. A balanced flow of Qi is essential for health, and disruptions in this flow can lead to various ailments, including hair loss.

Scientific Perspective: Modern science, while not directly addressing the concept of life force energy, recognizes the importance of nutrient density, antioxidants, and bioactive compounds found in whole foods. These components play a crucial role in cellular health, immune function, and reducing oxidative stress - factors that are directly linked to hair growth and health.

3.1.2 The Role of Life Force Energy in Hair Growth

Cellular Vitality: Life force energy is believed to enhance cellular vitality, which is essential for the active growth phase of the hair cycle (Anagen phase). Cells with abundant life force energy are better equipped to repair, regenerate, and support healthy hair follicles.

Immune System Support: A diet rich in life force energy supports and enriches the immune system, helping to protect hair follicles from autoimmune conditions like Alopecia areata.

Stress Reduction: Foods high in life force energy are also thought to reduce stress by supporting the nervous system, which in turn reduces cortisol levels a hormone known to contribute to hair thinning and loss.

3.2 The Impact of Diet on Hair Health

The saying "you are what you eat" holds especially true when it comes to hair health. The nutrients and life force energy present in your diet directly influence the strength, growth, and appearance of your hair. This section explores the key nutrients necessary for hair health and how to incorporate them into your diet.

3.2.1 Essential Nutrients for Hair Growth

Proteins: Hair is primarily composed of a protein called keratin. Adequate protein intake is essential for the production of keratin, which strengthens hair and promotes growth. Sources of high-quality protein include soybeans, sprouts, eggs, dairy products, legumes, and nuts.

Vitamins and Minerals:

Vitamin A: Essential for the production of sebum, a natural oil that moisturizes the scalp and keeps hair healthy. Rich sources include sweet potatoes, carrots, spinach, and kale.
B-Vitamins (Biotin): Biotin, or vitamin B7, is crucial for hair health. It helps produce keratin and supports hair follicle growth. Foods rich in biotin include eggs, almonds, and whole grains.
Vitamin C: Necessary for collagen production, which strengthens hair. Vitamin C also aids in iron absorption, a critical factor for preventing hair loss. Citrus fruits, strawberries, bell peppers, and broccoli are excellent sources.
Vitamin D: Plays a role in creating new hair follicles. A deficiency in vitamin D is linked to alopecia. The body produces vitamin D when exposed to sunlight, but it can also be obtained from fortified foods and fatty fish.
Iron: Iron is essential for red blood cell production, which transports oxygen to hair follicles. Iron deficiency can lead to anemia, a common cause of hair loss. Good sources of iron include spinach, lentils, and beans.
Zinc: Supports hair tissue growth and repair. It also keeps the oil glands around the follicles working properly. Foods rich in zinc include legumes, whole grains, pumpkin seeds, nuts and eggs.

3.2.2 Antioxidants and Their Role in Hair Health

Oxidative Stress and Hair Follicles: Oxidative stress, caused by free radicals, damages hair follicles and can lead to hair loss. Antioxidants neutralize free radicals, protecting hair follicles from damage. They also help maintain the health of the scalp, creating an optimal environment for hair growth.

Antioxidant-Rich Foods: Incorporating foods rich in antioxidants into your diet is crucial for combating oxidative stress. These foods include:

- **Berries:** Blueberries, strawberries, and raspberries are high in vitamins and flavonoids, potent antioxidants that protect against cellular damage.
- **Nuts and Seeds:** Almonds, walnuts, and flaxseeds are excellent sources of vitamin E, which has powerful antioxidant properties.
- **Leafy Greens:** Spinach and kale are packed with vitamins A and C, which support sebum production and collagen synthesis.
- **Green Tea:** Rich in polyphenols, green tea is a potent antioxidant that can help protect hair follicles.

3.2.3 The Role of Healthy Fats

Omega-3 Fatty Acids: Omega-3s are essential fats that the body cannot produce on its own. They reduce inflammation, nourish hair follicles, and promote scalp health. Foods rich in omega-3 fatty acids include fatty fish like salmon, chia seeds, walnuts, and flaxseeds.

Monounsaturated Fats: These healthy fats help maintain the moisture balance of the scalp and support overall hair health. Coconut oil, avocados, and nuts are excellent sources of monounsaturated fats.

3.3 Building a Diet Rich in Life Force Energy

To harness the life force energy in your diet, it's important to focus on foods that are fresh, whole, and minimally processed. These foods are closest to their natural state and are believed to contain the highest levels of life force energy.

3.3.1 Emphasizing Whole Foods

These should make up the bulk of your diet. They are rich in vitamins, minerals, antioxidants, and fiber, all of which are essential for hair health. Opt for organic produce, when possible, to avoid exposure to pesticides and to maximize nutrient content.

Whole Grains: Whole grains such as brown rice, jowar, bajra and oats are packed with B-vitamins, iron, and zinc, which support hair growth and overall health. Avoid refined grains, which are stripped of their nutrients and have a lower life force energy.

Lean Proteins: Choose high-quality sources of protein, including sprouts, pulses, eggs, legumes, and dairy. These foods provide the amino acids necessary for keratin production, which strengthens hair.

3.3.2 Avoiding Processed Foods

The Problem with Processed Foods: Processed foods are often stripped of their natural nutrients and are laden with additives, preservatives, and unhealthy fats. These foods are believed to have little to no life force energy and can contribute to poor health and hair loss.

Common Offenders: Sugary snacks, fast food, packaged meals, and sodas are all examples of processed foods that should be minimized or eliminated from your diet. These foods can lead to inflammation, oxidative stress, and nutrient deficiencies, all of which can negatively impact hair health.

Fresh Fruits and Vegetables:

3.3.3 Hydration and Hair Health

Water is essential for every cell in your body, including those that make up your hair follicles. Dehydration can lead to dry, brittle hair and a dry scalp, which can impede hair growth. Aim to drink at least 8-10 glasses of water per day.

Hydrating Foods: In addition to drinking water, you can also stay hydrated by eating water-rich foods like cucumbers, watermelon, oranges, and celery. These foods not only hydrate but also provide vitamins and minerals that support hair health.

The Importance of Water:

3.4 Practical Steps for Incorporating Life Force Energy into Your Diet

Incorporating life force energy into your diet doesn't have to be complicated. Here are some practical steps to help you get started:

3.4.1 Meal Planning for Hair Health

Balanced Meals: Plan meals that include a balance of protein, healthy fats, and complex carbohydrates. For example, a typical meal might include pulses and eggs (protein and omega-3s), rice, jowar or bajra (complex carbs and B-vitamins), and a side of steamed vegetables, capsicum, moringa, carrots & broccoli (vitamins A and C, fiber).

Incorporate Variety: Eating a wide variety of foods ensures that you get all the nutrients your body needs. Rotate your sources of protein, fruits, and vegetables to maximize nutrient intake and life force energy.

Cook at Home: Preparing your meals at home allows you to control the quality and freshness of the ingredients. It also enables you to avoid the unhealthy fats, sugars, and preservatives found in restaurant and processed foods. You must prepare the meal in remembrance of Supreme God and ask for blessings. You can play light spiritual music and keep giving vibrations of love and affection to the food while cooking at peace. Its highly recommended to keep smiling and avoid watching any electronic devices while cooking to enhance the life force energy of the food.

3.4.2 Superfoods for Hair Health

Sweet potatoes: Antioxidants vitamins and minerals including beta-carotene.
Carrots: filled with vitamin A - beta carotene, biotin, vitamin K1 and B6,
Avocado: Packed with healthy fats, vitamins E and C, and biotin, avocados are a hair superfood. Incorporate avocado into salads, smoothies, or eat it on its own as a snack.
Spinach: Spinach is rich in iron, vitamin A, and folate all essential

nutrients for hair growth. Add spinach to salads, soups, and smoothies for a nutrient boost.

Eggs: A powerhouse of protein, biotin, and other hair-healthy nutrients, eggs are a versatile and easy addition to your diet. Enjoy them boiled, scrambled, or as part of a healthy breakfast.

Nuts and Seeds: Almonds, walnuts, and chia seeds are rich in healthy fats, biotin, and zinc. Snack on nuts and seeds throughout the day or add them to your meals for an extra nutrient boost.

3.4.3 Detoxifying the Body for Healthy Hair

Liver Health: The liver plays a crucial role in detoxifying the body, and a well-functioning liver is essential for hair health. Foods that support liver health include garlic, turmeric, beets, and leafy greens.

Herbal Teas: Herbal teas like green tea, ginger tea are known for their detoxifying properties. They help cleanse the liver and kidneys, promoting better overall health and, by extension, healthier hair.

Intermittent Fasting: Intermittent fasting can give your digestive system a break and promote detoxification. It may also improve gut health and support hair growth by reducing inflammation and improving nutrient absorption.

3.5 The Connection Between Gut Health and Life Force Energy

As discussed in Chapter 2, the gut microbiome plays a critical role in hair health. The foods you consume not only provide nutrients but also influence the composition and health of your gut microbiome. A diet rich in life force energy supports a healthy gut, which in turn supports healthy body and mind and which in-turn promotes healthy hair.

3.5.1 Prebiotics and Probiotics in the Diet

Prebiotic Foods: Prebiotics are types of fiber that feed the beneficial bacteria in your gut. Foods like apples, bananas, garlic, onions, and asparagus are rich in prebiotics and should be included in your diet to support gut health and hair growth.

Probiotic Foods: Probiotics are live bacteria that help maintain a healthy gut microbiome. Fermented foods like yogurt, butter milk, kefir, sauerkraut, tempeh and kimchi are excellent sources of probiotics. Incorporating these foods into your diet can help ensure a balanced gut microbiome, which is essential for optimal nutrient absorption and hair health.

3.5.2 The Impact of Sugar on Gut and Hair Health

Sugar and Inflammation: High sugar intake can lead to inflammation, which can negatively impact both gut health and hair health. Sugar feeds harmful bacteria in the gut, leading to an imbalance that can affect nutrient absorption and hair growth.

Reducing Sugar Intake: To support gut and hair health, reduce your intake of added sugars. Focus on natural sweeteners like honey or maple syrup in moderation, and limit consumption of sugary snacks and beverages.

3.6 The Role of Mindful Eating in Hair Health

After we discussed mindful cooking, it is also important to have mindful eating habits. Mindful eating is the practice of being fully present and aware during meals, paying attention to the experience of eating and the signals your body sends about hunger and satiety. This practice not only improves digestion and nutrient absorption but also enhances your connection to the life force energy in your food. Before starting the meal, one must thank the Supreme God for providing the food for their life and then give positive vibrations to the food in your plate. This practice helps in increasing the life force energy of the food which you are about to consume.

3.6.1 Benefits of Mindful Eating

Improved Digestion: Eating slowly and mindfully allows your body to properly digest food, ensuring that you absorb the maximum nutrients needed for hair health.

Reduced Stress: Mindful eating helps reduce stress by promoting a calm and focused eating environment. Lower stress levels contribute to healthier hair by reducing the production of cortisol, a hormone linked to hair loss.

Better Food Choices: When you eat mindfully, you are more likely to make healthier food choices. You become more attuned to your body's needs and are less likely to overeat or consume unhealthy foods.

3.6.2 Practicing Mindful Eating

Set the Scene: Create a calm, distraction-free environment for meals. Turn off the TV, put away your phone, and focus solely on your meal.

Chew Thoroughly: Take time to chew your food thoroughly, which aids digestion and allows you to fully savor the flavors and textures of your food.

Listen to Your Body: Pay attention to your body's hunger and fullness cues. Eat until you are satisfied, not stuffed, and stop when you feel content.

3.7 Real-Life Applications and Success Stories

To bring these concepts to life, let's explore real-life applications and success stories from individuals who have transformed their hair health through diet and lifestyle changes.

3.7.1 Case Study: Reversing Hair Thinning with a Nutrient-Dense Diet

A 40-year-old woman experienced significant hair thinning due to chronic stress and a diet high in processed foods. After transitioning to a diet rich in whole foods, lean proteins, and antioxidant-rich fruits and vegetables, she noticed a marked improvement in her hair health within six months. Her hair became thicker, shinier, and less prone to breakage.

Key changes included incorporating more leafy greens, carrots ,tomatoes, almonds, walnuts, fruits, soybeans, sprouts, pulses and nuts into her diet, as well as reducing sugar intake and practicing mindful eating.

3.7.2 Practical Tips for Success

Start Small: Begin by making small, manageable changes to your diet. For example, swap out refined grains for whole grains or add an extra serving of vegetables to your meals.

Stay Consistent: Consistency is key to seeing results. Stick to your new dietary habits for several months to allow your body and your hair to fully benefit from the changes.

Track Your Progress: Keep a food journal to track what you eat and any changes you notice in your hair health. This can help you identify which foods work best for you and keep you motivated.

Conclusion

The foods you eat are more than just fuel for your body; they are the building blocks of your health, vitality, and beauty, including your hair. By embracing a diet rich in life force energy, you can nourish your hair from the inside out, promoting growth, strength, and shine. A diet full of life force energy elevates your consciousness, helps you harmonize with nature and connects you to high consciousness of the universe. As you continue this journey, remember that true hair health comes from a holistic approach that combines diet, lifestyle, and mindful practices.

In the next chapter, we will explore the power of morning rituals, including the benefits of early morning walks, which can further enhance your journey to healthy, vibrant hair.

CHAPTER FOUR

THE POWER OF MORNING RITUALS

Morning rituals are powerful tools that can set the tone for your entire day, influencing your mood, energy levels, consciousness and even your hair health. By starting your day with intentional practices that nurture your mind and body, you can create a positive ripple effect that benefits every aspect of your life, including the health and vitality of your hair. This chapter explores the importance of establishing morning rituals, particularly focusing on the benefits of early morning walks, and provides practical guidance on how to incorporate these practices into your daily routine.

4.1 The Science Behind Morning Rituals

Morning rituals are more than just a series of actions; they are habits that, when practiced consistently, can lead to significant improvements in mental and physical well-being. These rituals help to align your body's natural rhythms with the day's cycle, connect with the nature, promote a sense of balance and harmony that is essential for overall health, including hair health. Its helps you to connect your soul to your body at a better level. Its like connecting the software to hardware of an electronic device at a much efficient level to get better output.

4.1.1 The Role of Circadian Rhythms

Understanding Circadian Rhythms: Circadian rhythms are the natural, internal processes that regulate the sleep-wake cycle and repeat roughly every 24 hours. These rhythms influence various biological functions, including hormone production, digestion, and cellular repair, all of which impact hair growth and health.

Morning Light and Melatonin: Exposure to natural light in the morning helps regulate the production of melatonin, a hormone that governs sleep. Melatonin also plays a role in hair growth by supporting the hair follicle's anagen phase. By aligning your morning activities with your circadian rhythms, you can enhance your body's natural processes, leading to better hair health.

4.1.2 Hormonal Balance and Stress Reduction

Cortisol Awakening Response: Cortisol, often referred to as the stress hormone, follows a daily pattern where its levels peak in the early morning and gradually decrease throughout the day. Engaging in morning rituals like walking and meditation can help regulate cortisol levels, reducing stress and its negative impact on hair growth.

The Role of Endorphins: Physical activities, such as walking, trigger the release of endorphins - hormones that promote feelings of well-being and reduce stress. Lower stress levels are associated with a reduction in hair loss conditions like Telogen effluvium and Alopecia areata.

4.2 The Benefits of Early Morning Walks

One of the most beneficial morning rituals for overall health and hair vitality is the early morning brisk walk before breakfast in the midst of nature. This simple yet powerful practice offers a myriad of health benefits, ranging from improved circulation to enhanced mood, all of which contribute to healthier hair.

4.2.1 Boosting Circulation

Improved Blood Flow to Hair Follicles: Walking increases your heart rate within healthy range, which boosts circulation throughout your body, including your scalp.
Better blood flow means that your hair follicles receive more oxygen and

essential nutrients, supporting stronger and faster hair growth.

Enhanced Nutrient Delivery: The improved circulation from walking also ensures that the nutrients you consume in your diet are efficiently delivered to your hair follicles. This is crucial for maintaining the anagen phase of the hair growth cycle and preventing hair thinning.

4.2.2 Balancing Hormones

Regulating Cortisol Levels: As mentioned earlier, morning walks help regulate cortisol levels. By keeping cortisol in check, you reduce the likelihood of stress-induced hair loss, a common issue in today's fast-paced world.

Stimulating Serotonin Production: Exposure to natural sunlight during a morning walk increases serotonin levels a hormone that stabilizes mood and promotes feelings of happiness. Serotonin also indirectly supports hair health by reducing stress and improving sleep quality.

4.2.3 Enhancing Mental Clarity and Focus

Mental Benefits of Walking: Walking, especially in the morning, can clear your mind, boost creativity, and enhance focus. This mental clarity can reduce stress and anxiety, both of which are known to negatively impact hair health.

Mind-Body Connection: Engaging in a morning walk helps strengthen the mind-body connection. This holistic approach to health ensures that your mental state positively influences your physical well-being, including the health of your hair.

4.2.4 Promoting Better Sleep

Sunlight and Sleep Quality: Exposure to natural sunlight in the morning helps set your body's internal clock, making it easier to fall asleep at night. Quality sleep is crucial for hair health, as most of the body's repair and growth processes occur during sleep.

Melatonin Production: As morning sunlight helps regulate melatonin production, it supports a healthy sleep cycle, ensuring that your body and your hair follicles have the time needed to repair and regenerate.

4.3 Establishing a Morning Walk Routine

Creating a consistent morning walk routine is essential for reaping the full benefits of this practice. Whether you are a beginner or someone looking to enhance your current routine, this section provides practical tips for establishing and maintaining a morning walk habit.

4.3.1 Starting Small and Building Consistency

Begin with Short Walks: If you're new to morning walks, start with short, manageable distances perhaps 10 to 15 minutes. The key is consistency, so focus on making this a daily habit rather than worrying about the duration or intensity.

Gradually Increase Duration: As you become more comfortable with your routine, gradually increase the duration of your walks. Aim to reach 45 minutes of walking each morning, which is optimal for improving circulation, reducing stress, and supporting hair health.

4.3.2 Choosing the Right Environment

Walking Outdoors vs. Indoors: Walking outdoors, particularly in natural settings, offers additional benefits such as exposure to fresh air and sunlight, both of which enhance the positive effects on your mental and physical health. If walking outdoors is not feasible, walking on a treadmill or in a well-lit indoor space is still beneficial.

Selecting a Scenic Route: Choose a walking route that you enjoy. Scenic paths through parks, along the beach, or in your neighborhood can make the experience more enjoyable and increase your likelihood of sticking with the routine.

4.3.3 Incorporating Mindfulness into Your Walk

Mindful Walking Practices: Turn your morning walk into a mindfulness practice by focusing on your breath, the sensations in your body, and the environment around you. This can enhance the stress-relieving benefits of walking and further promote hair health.

Walking Meditation: Walking meditation is walking in remembrance of the Supreme Soul and involves focusing on the rhythm of your steps and your breath as you walk. This practice not only calms the mind but also strengthens the mind-body connection, which is vital for holistic health and hair wellness.

4.3.4 Overcoming Common Barriers

Weather Challenges: Weather conditions can sometimes make outdoor walking difficult. On rainy or cold days, consider walking indoors or using a treadmill. Alternatively, invest in weather-appropriate clothing to keep your walks comfortable year-round.

Time Constraints: If time is a constraint, consider breaking your walk into shorter sessions throughout the day. However, a morning walk is ideal for setting a positive tone for the day, so try to prioritize this time as much as possible.

Motivation: Maintaining motivation can be challenging, especially on days when you feel tired or unmotivated. Setting small goals, finding a walking partner, or listening to music or podcasts can help keep you motivated.

4.4 Additional Morning Rituals for Hair Health

While a morning walk is a cornerstone of a healthy morning routine, incorporating other rituals can further enhance your overall well-being and hair health. This section explores complementary practices that can be seamlessly integrated into your morning routine.

4.4.1 Meditation:

Benefits for Hair Health: Meditation in the morning not only helps you to attain higher consciousness but also help to harmonize the endocrine hormones released by the body. Ideal time to meditate is around 4 AM - 5 AM. However, you can meditate at any time in the morning if you're not able to get up at 4 AM. Make sure you meditate within 10-15 mins immediately after getting up in morning. This simple yet strong routine will help you increase your coping ability to fight stress, helps you attain mental peace. Raj yoga is a simple form of meditation which can be practiced. It will be covered in detail in following chapters.

4.4.2 Yoga and Stretching

Benefits for Hair Health: Yoga and stretching in the morning help increase circulation, reduce stress, and balance hormones - all of which contribute to healthy hair. Certain yoga poses, such as downward dog and headstands, specifically increase blood flow to the scalp, promoting hair growth.

Incorporating Yoga into Your Routine: Consider dedicating 10-15 minutes after your walk to a yoga or stretching routine. This can help release any tension built up during your walk and further enhance the flow of life force energy throughout your body.

4.4.3 Morning Hydration

Start Your Day with Water: Hydration is crucial for maintaining the health of your hair and scalp. Begin your morning with a glass of warm water, perhaps with a slice of lemon for added vitamin C and honey for better taste and potential detoxification benefits.

Hydrating Foods: Incorporate hydrating foods into your morning routine, such as fresh fruits like watermelon, oranges, or cucumbers, to further support your body's hydration needs.

4.4.4 Mindful Eating

Breakfast and Hair Health: A nutritious breakfast sets the foundation for your day. Focus on a balanced meal that includes protein, healthy fats, and complex carbohydrates. Foods like sprouts, beans, multigrain porridge, eggs, avocado, whole grains, and berries provide essential nutrients that support hair health.

Mindful Eating Practices: Eating mindfully in the morning- free from distractions helps improve digestion and ensures that your body absorbs the nutrients needed for hair growth and overall health.

4.4.5 Journaling and Gratitude Practice

Mental Health and Hair Growth: The health of your hair is closely tied to your mental well-being. Starting your day with a gratitude journal or a brief reflection on positive thoughts can help reduce stress and promote a positive mindset, both of which are beneficial for hair health.

Setting Intentions: Use this time to set positive intentions for the day. Whether it's focusing on self-care, increasing coping ability to manage stress, or making healthy food choices with higher life force energy, setting an intention helps guide your actions throughout the day.

4.5 The Long-Term Benefits of Morning Rituals

The most important step for successful outcome of any idea or ritual is execution. Once you have executed the ritual in your life, Consistency is key to reap maximum benefit. Over time, these practices can lead to significant improvements in your physical, mental, and hair health. This section explores the long-term benefits you can expect from maintaining a morning routine.

4.5.1 Sustained Energy and Vitality

Increased Energy Levels: Regular morning rituals, such as meditation, walking and yoga, help maintain high energy levels throughout the day. This sustained energy supports all bodily functions, including those critical for hair growth. The higher coping ability also helps you to respond to external pressures in a more meaningful manner and reduce stress, rather than an anxious reaction to pressure - creating stress in life.

Enhanced Metabolism: Morning physical activities boost your metabolism, which aids in nutrient absorption and overall health. A well-functioning metabolism ensures that your hair follicles receive the nutrients they need to thrive.

4.5.2 Improved Hair Growth and Strength

Stronger Hair: Consistent morning rituals that promote circulation and reduce stress can lead to stronger, healthier hair over time. Many people report reduced hair shedding and increased hair thickness after incorporating these practices into their daily routine.

Healthy Scalp: Morning rituals that include hydration, mindfulness, and proper nutrition contribute to a healthy scalp, which is essential for maintaining and promoting hair growth.

4.5.3 Mental Clarity and Emotional Well-Being

Reduced Anxiety and Depression: The combination of physical activity, mindfulness, and gratitude in the morning helps reduce anxiety and depression, both of which are linked to hair loss. A positive mental state supports overall well-being and contributes to healthier hair.

Better Stress Management: By starting your day with stress-reducing practices, you equip yourself with the tools needed to handle daily challenges with greater ease. This resilience to stress not only benefits your mental health but also your hair.

4.5.4 Longevity and Quality of Life

Overall, Health Benefits: Morning rituals that promote physical activity, mindfulness, and proper nutrition contribute to longevity and a higher quality of life. These practices support cardiovascular health, mental clarity, and immune function, all of which are linked to hair health.

Holistic Approach to Health: By consistently practicing morning rituals, you cultivate a holistic approach to health that benefits every aspect of your life, including your appearance, energy levels, and emotional well-being.

4.6 Real-Life Applications and Success Stories

To illustrate the transformative power of morning rituals, let's explore real-life applications and success stories from individuals who have significantly improved their hair health and overall well-being through consistent morning practices.

4.6.1 Case Study: From Hair Thinning to Hair Thriving

A 45-year-old man experienced significant hair thinning due to chronic stress and an inconsistent lifestyle. After committing to a daily morning walk, along with mindfulness and hydration practices, he noticed not only a reduction in hair shedding but also an improvement in hair density and overall scalp health.

Over the course of a year, his hair continued to improve, becoming thicker and stronger. Additionally, he reported enhanced mental clarity, reduced stress, and better sleep quality - all of which contributed to his improved hair health.

4.6.2 Practical Tips for Success

Start with One Ritual: If you're new to morning rituals, start with just one practice, such as a morning walk, and gradually add others as you become more comfortable.

Track Your Progress: Keep a journal to track how you feel after your morning rituals, as well as any changes in your hair health. This can help you stay motivated and adjust your routine as needed.

Celebrate Small Wins: Recognize and celebrate small improvements in your hair health and overall well-being. This positive reinforcement will help you stay committed to your morning routine.

Conclusion

Morning rituals are powerful tools that can significantly improve your overall health and hair vitality. By incorporating practices such as early morning meditation, walks, yoga, proper hydration, and a balanced nutritious breakfast having high life force energy, you can create a foundation for healthy, thriving hair. As you establish these rituals, remember that consistency is key. Over time, these practices will not only enhance your hair health but also contribute to a more balanced, energized, and fulfilling life.

In the next chapter, we will delve into the specific yoga practices that can further support hair health, exploring how ancient techniques can be applied to modern life for optimal well-being.

CHAPTER FIVE

YOGA FOR HAIR HEALTH

Yoga, an ancient practice that combines physical postures, breathing exercises, and meditation, offers a holistic approach to health and wellness. While yoga is widely known for its benefits in improving flexibility, strength, and mental clarity, it also has profound effects on hair health. This chapter explores how specific yoga practices can enhance circulation, reduce stress, balance hormones, and ultimately support healthier hair growth.

5.1 The Connection Between Yoga and Hair Health

Yoga's impact on hair health stems from its ability to improve overall physical and mental well-being. By addressing the root causes of hair loss, such as poor circulation, high stress levels, and hormonal imbalances, yoga helps create an environment conducive to healthy hair growth.

5.1.1 Enhancing Circulation

Blood Flow to the Scalp: Yoga poses, particularly those that involve inversions (where the head is below the heart), help increase blood flow to the scalp. This enhanced circulation delivers more oxygen and essential nutrients to the hair follicles, promoting stronger, healthier hair.

Oxygen and Nutrient Delivery: Better circulation ensures that the hair follicles receive a steady supply of the nutrients required for hair growth. This is crucial for maintaining the anagen phase, the active growth phase of the hair cycle.

5.1.2 Reducing Stress and Anxiety

The Stress-Hair Loss Connection: Chronic stress is a significant contributor to hair loss conditions such as Telogen effluvium and Alopecia areata. Yoga's emphasis on deep breathing and relaxation helps lower cortisol levels, the hormone associated with stress, thereby reducing hair loss.

Yoga's Calming Effect: Through mindfulness and meditation, yoga fosters a sense of inner peace and relaxation, which directly benefits hair health by minimizing the impact of stress on the body.

5.1.3 Balancing Hormones

Hormonal Imbalances and Hair Loss: Conditions such as thyroid dysfunction, polycystic ovary syndrome (PCOS), and menopause can lead to hormonal imbalances that affect hair growth. Yoga helps regulate the endocrine system, promoting hormonal balance and reducing the risk of hair loss related to these conditions.

Influence on Endocrine Glands: Certain yoga poses stimulate the endocrine glands, such as the thyroid, pituitary, and adrenal glands, which play a key role in regulating hormones that affect hair growth.

5.2 Key Yoga Poses for Hair Health

Incorporating specific yoga poses into your daily routine can significantly improve hair health. These poses, chosen for their ability to boost circulation, reduce stress, and balance hormones, are easy to practice and can be performed by individuals of all fitness levels. Its very important to seek expert guidance from a trained certified yoga teacher before exploring these yoga asanas.

5.2.1 Sirsasana (Headstand)

How It Helps: Sirsasana is known as the "king of asanas" because of its numerous health benefits. By inverting the body, this pose directs blood flow to the scalp, enhancing oxygen and nutrient delivery to the hair follicles. It also helps relieve stress and anxiety, both of which can contribute to hair loss.

How to Perform Sirsasana:

- Start by kneeling on the floor and interlacing your fingers to create a firm base for your head.
- Place the crown of your head on the floor with your hands cradling the back of your head.
- Slowly lift your knees off the floor, straighten your legs, and walk your feet closer to your head.
- Engage your core and lift your feet off the floor, bringing your legs up into a straight line above your head.
- Hold the pose for 30 seconds to a minute, then slowly lower your legs back down.

Modifications : Beginners can perform this pose against a wall for support, or practice the preparatory pose, Dolphin Pose, which also enhances blood flow to the scalp without the full inversion.

5.2.2 Sarvangasana (Shoulder Stand)

How It Helps: Sarvangasana, or Shoulder Stand, is another inversion that promotes blood flow to the scalp. This pose also stimulates the thyroid gland, helping to balance hormones that influence hair growth.

How to Perform Sarvangasana:

- Lie on your back with your arms by your sides, palms facing down.
- Slowly lift your legs towards the ceiling, using your abdominal muscles.
- Place your hands on your lower back for support and lift your hips off the floor, stacking your hips over your shoulders.

- Keep your legs straight and your toes pointed towards the ceiling.
- Hold the pose for 1 to 3 minutes, then slowly lower your legs back down to the floor.

Modifications : Beginners can use a folded blanket under the shoulders to support the neck, or practice the Legs-Up-the-Wall Pose, which offers similar benefits with less strain.

5.2.3 Adho Mukha Svanasana (Downward-Facing Dog)

How It Helps: Adho Mukha Svanasana is a foundational yoga pose that improves circulation to the scalp while stretching and strengthening the entire body. This pose also helps relieve tension in the shoulders and neck, areas where stress often accumulates.

How to Perform Adho Mukha Svanasana:

- Start on your hands and knees, with your wrists aligned under your shoulders and your knees under your hips.
- Spread your fingers wide and press firmly into your hands.
- Tuck your toes under and lift your hips towards the ceiling, straightening your legs.
- Keep your head between your arms, looking towards your knees or navel.
- Hold the pose for 1 to 3 minutes, focusing on your breath and the stretch in your back and legs.

Modifications : Beginners can bend their knees slightly to avoid straining the hamstrings, or use a yoga block under their hands for added support.

5.2.4 Uttanasana (Standing Forward Bend)

How It Helps: Uttanasana is a gentle inversion that helps increase blood flow to the scalp while calming the mind and relieving stress. This pose also stretches the hamstrings and lower back, promoting overall flexibility and relaxation.

How to Perform Uttanasana:

- Stand with your feet hip-width apart and your hands on your hips.
- Inhale deeply, then exhale as you hinge at your hips, bringing your torso towards your legs.
- Let your head hang heavy, and place your hands on the floor, your shins, or hold opposite elbows.
- Relax your neck and shoulders, and allow your breath to deepen. Hold the pose for 1 to 2 minutes, then slowly roll up to standing on an inhale.

Modifications : If you have tight hamstrings, you can bend your knees slightly or use a yoga block to rest your hands.

5.2.5 Vajrasana (Thunderbolt Pose) with Pranayama

How It Helps: Vajrasana is a seated pose that is often combined with pranayama (breathing exercises) to enhance relaxation and reduce stress. This pose stimulates the digestive organs, improving nutrient absorption, which is vital for healthy hair.

How to Perform Vajrasana with Pranayama:

- Kneel on the floor with your knees together and sit back on your heels, with your spine straight and hands resting on your thighs.
- Close your eyes and focus on your breath.
- Begin with deep abdominal breathing, inhaling deeply through your nose, allowing your belly to expand.
- Exhale slowly and completely, feeling your belly contract.
- Continue this breathing pattern for 5 to 10 minutes, focusing on relaxation and the flow of breath.

Modifications : If sitting on your heels is uncomfortable, place a cushion or folded blanket under your hips for support.

There are few more asanas which you can gradually incorporate in your morning ritual activity of yoga. As you get consistent with yoga routine, you can explore more and more variations to get optimal benefits.

5.2.6 Balasana (Child's Pose): Reduces stress and promotes relaxation, which can prevent stress-related hair loss.

5.2.7 Matsyasana (Fish Pose): This back-bending pose helps stimulate the thyroid gland, which plays a crucial role in hair growth. It also promotes healthy digestion and circulation, both of which are important for scalp and hair health.

5.2.8 Pavanamuktasana (Wind-Relieving Pose): This pose aids digestion and removes toxins from the body, which can improve the absorption of hair-nourishing nutrients.

5.2.9 Setu Bandhasana (Bridge Pose): Bridge Pose opens up the chest and increases blood flow to the scalp and brain, promoting hair growth by ensuring the scalp receives vital nutrients and oxygen.

5.2.10 Paschimottanasana (Seated Forward Bend): This calming forward bend enhances circulation to the scalp, improves digestion, and reduces stress, making it effective for hair health.

5.3 Pranayama (Breathing Exercises) for Hair Health

Pranayama, the practice of controlled breathing, is an integral part of yoga that offers numerous benefits for hair health. By calming the mind, reducing stress, and enhancing oxygenation, pranayama supports the overall health of the body, including the scalp and hair follicles.

5.3.1 Anulom vilom (Alternate Nostril Breathing)

How It Helps: Anulom vilom balances the nervous system, reduces stress, and improves oxygenation. This breathing technique also enhances the flow of prana (life force energy), promoting overall vitality and hair health.

How to Perform Anulom vilom:

- Sit comfortably in a cross-legged position with your spine straight and shoulders relaxed.
- Close your right nostril with your right thumb and inhale deeply through your left nostril.
- Close your left nostril with your right ring finger and exhale through your right nostril.
- Inhale deeply through your right nostril, then close it and exhale through your left nostril.

This completes one round. Continue for 5 to 10 minutes, focusing on the breath and the calming effects of the practice.

5.3.2 Kapalabhati (Skull Shining Breath)

How It Helps: Kapalabhati is an energizing breathing technique that detoxifies the body, improves circulation, and enhances digestion. The increased oxygenation and circulation support hair follicle health and promote hair growth.

How to Perform Kapalabhati:

- Sit in a comfortable seated position with your spine straight and hands resting on your knees.
- Take a deep inhale, then exhale forcefully through your nose while contracting your abdominal muscles.
- Allow the inhalation to occur passively, and continue with forceful exhalations at a steady rhythm.
- Perform 20 to 30 breaths, then take a deep inhale and exhale slowly. Repeat for 3 to 5 rounds

  Modifications : Beginners should start slowly, with fewer breaths per round, and gradually increase the pace as they become more comfortable.

5.3.3 Bhramari (Bee Breath)

How It Helps: Bhramari, or Bee Breath, is a calming pranayama technique that reduces stress and anxiety by soothing the nervous system. This technique also improves circulation to the scalp, supporting hair health.

How to Perform Bhramari:

- Sit in a comfortable seated position with your eyes closed and hands resting on your knees.
- Take a deep inhale through your nose, then exhale slowly while making a humming sound like a bee.
- Focus on the vibrations created by the sound and the relaxation they bring to your mind and body.
- Continue for 5 to 10 minutes, feeling the stress and tension melt away with each breath.

There are few more pranayama which you can gradually incorporate in your morning ritual activity of yoga.

5.3.4Udgeeth Pranayama (Chanting Breath): This technique focuses on chanting "Om," which helps calm the mind, reduce stress, and promote inner peace. It relieves mental tension, which is often a key contributor to hair loss.

5.3.5 Sheetali Pranayama (Cooling Breath): This cooling pranayama helps regulate body temperature and reduce heat in the body, which can prevent hair fall related to excessive body heat and stress.

5.3.6 Ujjayi Pranayama (Ocean Breath): This technique improves oxygenation throughout the body, including the scalp, and induces a calming effect that can reduce stress-related hair loss.

5.3.7 Surya Bhedana (Right Nostril Breathing): Stimulating the right nostril enhances energy levels and promotes good digestion, both of which are vital for delivering nutrients to hair follicles.

5.4 Developing a Yoga Practice for Hair Health

To fully benefit from the positive effects of yoga on hair health, it's important to develop a consistent practice. This section provides guidance on how to create a sustainable yoga routine that supports your overall well-being and hair growth.

5.4.1 Setting Up a Home Practice

Designate a quiet, clutter-free area in your home for yoga practice. This space should be inviting and comfortable, encouraging you to practice regularly.

Essential Equipment: Invest in a good-quality yoga mat, blocks, and straps to support your practice. These tools can help you achieve proper alignment and make poses more accessible.

5.4.2 Integrating Yoga into Your Daily Routine

Morning Practice: Incorporating yoga into your morning routine is an excellent way to start the day with a calm mind and energized body. Begin with a few poses and pranayama exercises, gradually building up to a full practice.

Evening Practice: Yoga can also be a powerful tool for unwinding in the evening. Focus on restorative poses and deep breathing exercises to release the stress of the day and prepare for restful sleep.

5.4.3 Balancing Yoga with Other Activities

Complementary Practices: Combine your yoga practice with other healthy habits, such as morning walks, meditation, and a balanced diet, to maximize the benefits for your hair and overall health.

Listening to Your Body: It's important to listen to your body and practice yoga at a pace that feels comfortable for you. Avoid pushing yourself too hard, as this can lead to injury and negate the benefits of the practice. Start under the supervision of some expert yoga teacher for better outcome and to avoid injuries.

5.5 Success Stories and Real-Life Applications

The transformative power of yoga for hair health is evident in the experiences of those who have incorporated these practices into their lives. This section highlights real-life success stories and offers practical tips for making yoga a part of your daily routine.

5.5.1 Case Study: Regaining Hair Health Through Yoga

Creating a Dedicated Space:

A 38-year-old woman experiencing hair thinning due to high stress levels and hormonal imbalances began practicing yoga regularly. She focused on poses that enhanced circulation and reduced stress, such as Sirsasana and Sarvangasana, combined with pranayama exercises like Anulom vilom and Bhramari.

Over six months, she noticed significant improvements in her hair health, including reduced shedding and increased hair density. Her overall well-being also improved, with less stress and better sleep.

5.5.2 Practical Tips for Success

Start Slowly: If you're new to yoga, begin with a few simple poses and gradually increase the complexity and duration of your practice. **Consistency is more important than intensity.**
Seek Guidance: Consider taking a few classes with a certified yoga instructor to learn proper alignment and technique. This will help you avoid injury and get the most out of your practice.
Stay Committed: The benefits of yoga for hair health are cumulative and become more apparent over time. Stay committed to your practice, and be patient as you wait for results.

Conclusion

Yoga offers a holistic approach to improving hair health by addressing the underlying causes of hair loss, such as poor circulation, stress, and hormonal imbalances. By incorporating specific yoga poses and pranayama exercises into your daily routine, you can enhance the health and vitality of your hair while also improving your overall well-being. As you continue your journey towards healthy, thriving hair, remember that yoga is a practice, not a quick fix. With patience, consistency, and dedication, the benefits will unfold, transforming not only your hair but also your life.

In the next chapter, we will explore the power of Raj Yoga meditation for inner peace, further delving into how mental and emotional well-being plays a crucial role in maintaining healthy hair.

CHAPTER SIX

Raj Yoga Meditation for Inner Peace and Hair Health

In the quest for healthy hair, the mind plays a more critical role than many realize. Stress, anxiety, and other mental health issues can significantly contribute to hair loss and poor hair health. Raj Yoga, a form of meditation focused on mental and spiritual peace, offers a powerful tool to cultivate inner calm and enhance overall well-being, which in turn supports hair health. This chapter delves into the practice of Raj Yoga meditation, its benefits for mental and emotional health, and how it can positively impact hair growth and vitality.

6.1 Understanding Raj Yoga Meditation

Raj Yoga, often referred to as the "King of Yogas," is a comprehensive practice that encompasses not just physical postures but also mental discipline and spiritual development. Unlike other forms of yoga that focus heavily on physical exercises, Raj Yoga emphasizes the mind and its ability to achieve a state of inner peace and self-realization.

6.1.1 The Philosophy of Raj Yoga

Roots in Ancient Texts: Raj Yoga is rooted in the ancient Indian scriptures, particularly the Yoga Sutras of Patanjali. It is considered the path of meditation and the highest form of yoga, aiming to unite the individual soul with the universal consciousness.

Eightfold Path: Raj Yoga is often associated with the Eightfold Path (Ashtanga), which includes ethical principles (yamas and niyamas), physical postures (asanas), breath control (pranayama), sense withdrawal (pratyahara), concentration (dharana), meditation (dhyana), and ultimately, spiritual absorption or enlightenment (samadhi).

Focus on Mind Control: The central aim of Raj Yoga is to control the fluctuations of the mind, leading to a state of mental clarity, emotional stability, and deep inner peace. This mental discipline is crucial for reducing stress and promoting overall health, including hair health.

6.1.2 The Mind-Body Connection in Raj Yoga

Stress and Hair Loss: Stress is a major contributor to hair loss conditions such as Telogen effluvium, where hair prematurely enters the resting phase and falls out in large amounts. Raj Yoga meditation helps mitigate the effects of stress by promoting relaxation, increases coping ability and reduces cortisol levels, the stress hormone associated with hair loss.

Mental Clarity and Focus: By training the mind to focus and achieve a state of calm, Raj Yoga meditation improves overall mental clarity. This clarity helps individuals make healthier lifestyle choices, including better dietary habits, focuses more on increasing the life force energy of diet, regular exercise, and proper hair care practices.

Emotional Well-Being: Emotional well-being is directly linked to hair health. Negative emotions such as anxiety, anger, and depression can disrupt the body's hormonal balance, leading to hair thinning and loss. Raj Yoga helps manage these emotions, fostering a sense of balance and harmony that supports healthy hair growth.

6.2 The Benefits of Raj Yoga Meditation for Hair Health

Practicing Raj Yoga meditation offers a range of benefits that extend beyond mental peace and spiritual growth. These benefits are directly connected to the health and vitality of your hair, making Raj Yoga an essential practice for anyone looking to improve their hair health.

6.2.1 Stress Reduction

Lowering Cortisol Levels: Cortisol, known as the "stress hormone," has a catabolic effect on the body, breaking down tissues, including hair follicles. High cortisol levels are linked to hair thinning and hair loss. Raj Yoga meditation helps lower cortisol levels, reducing the impact of stress on hair health.

Promoting Relaxation: Regular practice of Raj Yoga induces a deep state of relaxation, helping to alleviate the physical and emotional tensions that contribute to hair loss. This relaxation not only benefits the mind but also the body, promoting an environment conducive to healthy hair growth. It also helps in increasing the coping ability of an individual, which helps in tackling the external pressures of life. Coping ability of an individual is inversely proportional to stress.

6.2.2 Hormonal Balance

Regulating the Endocrine System: Raj Yoga meditation has a balancing effect on the endocrine system, which regulates hormones like cortisol, thyroid hormones, and sex hormones, all of which play a significant role in hair health. By promoting hormonal balance, Raj Yoga helps prevent hair loss related to hormonal imbalances.

Improving Sleep Quality: Good sleep is essential for maintaining hormonal balance. Raj Yoga meditation promotes better sleep by calming the nervous system and reducing stress. Improved sleep quality releases more of melatonin which allows the body to repair and regenerate, including hair follicles.

6.2.3 Enhanced Blood Circulation

Circulation and Hair Growth: While Raj Yoga primarily focuses on the mind, the deep breathing techniques involved in meditation also improve blood circulation throughout the body, including the scalp. Better circulation ensures that hair follicles receive the oxygen and nutrients needed for healthy growth.

Supporting Scalp Health: Improved circulation not only nourishes hair follicles but also helps maintain a healthy scalp, preventing issues like dryness, dandruff, and inflammation that can inhibit hair growth.

6.2.4 Strengthening the Immune System

Immune Function and Hair Health: Raj Yoga meditation has been shown to boost immune function by reducing stress and promoting overall health. A strong immune system is crucial for protecting hair follicles from autoimmune conditions like Alopecia areata, where the immune system mistakenly attacks hair follicles.

Reducing Inflammation: Chronic inflammation can damage hair follicles and lead to hair loss. Raj Yoga meditation helps reduce inflammation by lowering stress levels and promoting a state of inner peace, which supports healthier hair.

6.3 The Practice of Raj Yoga Meditation

To fully benefit from Raj Yoga, it's important to develop a consistent meditation practice. This section provides step-by-step guidance on how to practice Raj Yoga meditation, focusing on techniques that are particularly beneficial for hair health.

6.3.1 Preparing for Meditation

Creating a Quiet Space: Find a quiet, comfortable space where you can meditate without distractions. This could be a corner of your home or a dedicated meditation room. Ensure that the space is clean, uncluttered, and has a calming atmosphere.

Comfortable Seating: Sit in a comfortable position, either on a chair or on the floor with a cushion. The traditional posture for Raj Yoga is Sukhasana (Easy Pose), where you sit cross-legged with your spine straight and your hands resting on your knees. If sitting cross-legged is uncomfortable, sitting on a chair with your feet flat on the ground is perfectly acceptable.

Proper Posture: Maintaining good posture is important in Raj Yoga meditation. Keep your spine straight, your shoulders relaxed, and your head aligned with your spine. This posture helps maintain alertness while allowing your body to relax.

6.3.2 Focusing the Mind

Breath Awareness: Begin by focusing on your breath. Inhale deeply and exhale slowly, allowing your breath to naturally lengthen and deepen. Pay attention to the sensation of the breath as it enters and leaves your nostrils, or the rise and fall of your chest or abdomen. This focus on breath helps anchor your mind and prepares you for deeper meditation.

Mantra Meditation: Mantra meditation is a common practice in Raj Yoga. Choose a mantra - a word or phrase that resonates with you and repeat it silently or aloud during your meditation. Common mantras include "Om," "So Hum" (meaning "I am that"), or "Aham Brahmasmi" (meaning "I am the universe"). The repetition of the mantra helps calm the mind and deepen your meditative state.

Visualization: Visualization techniques can also be used to enhance your meditation. Visualize a peaceful scene, such as a calm ocean or a beautiful forest, or imagine a bright light at your heart center radiating warmth and peace throughout your body. Visualization helps you connect with positive emotions and a sense of inner calm. You can visualize yourself as a bright light like a star (soul consciousness) on your forehead in between the two eyebrow and connect it to Supreme soul in heaven. You can then visualize absorbing energy of knowledge, love, purity, peace, happiness, bliss and power (virtues of a soul) from the Supreme soul. This practice is very soothing and relaxes your subconscious mind, which in turn calms the conscious mind and relieves stress. It is a very powerful mode of Raj Yoga. I personally follow this Raj Yoga meditation and found it very useful.

6.3.3 Deepening the Meditation

Dhyana (Meditative Absorption): Once your mind is calm and focused, allow yourself to enter a state of Dhyana, or meditative absorption. In this state, you are fully immersed in the present moment, free from thoughts and distractions. This deep state of meditation is where the most profound healing occurs, as your mind and body are in perfect harmony.

Samadhi (State of Oneness): With regular practice, you may experience moments of Samadhi, a state of complete oneness with the universe. In this state, the boundaries between the self and the external world dissolve, leading to a profound sense of peace and enlightenment. While Samadhi is the ultimate goal of Raj Yoga, it is a state that is reached through consistent and dedicated practice.

6.3.4 Closing the Meditation

Gradual Transition: As you complete your meditation session, begin to slowly bring your awareness back to your body and surroundings. Wiggle your fingers and toes, stretch your arms and legs, and take a few deep breaths to re-energize your body.

Setting an Intention: Before you end your session, take a moment to set a positive intention for the day or week ahead. This intention can be related to your hair health, overall well-being, or any other aspect of your life. Setting an intention helps reinforce the positive energy generated during meditation and carries it forward into your daily life.

Expressing Gratitude: Conclude your meditation by expressing gratitude. Thank yourself for taking the time to meditate, and acknowledge the positive impact it will have on your mind, body, and hair health. Gratitude helps cultivate a positive mindset, which is essential for overall well-being.

6.4 Integrating Raj Yoga Meditation into Daily Life

For Raj Yoga meditation to have a lasting impact on your hair health and overall well-being, it's important to integrate it into your daily life. This section provides practical tips for incorporating meditation into your routine and making it a consistent practice.

6.4.1 Establishing a Routine

Morning Meditation: Starting your day with Raj Yoga meditation sets a positive tone for the day ahead. Morning meditation helps calm the mind, reduce stress, and prepare you for the challenges of the day. Ideal time to meditate is between 4 AM to 5AM, but even a brief 10 to 15 minute session at any time in the morning immediately after waking up can have significant benefits.

Evening Meditation: An evening meditation session can help you unwind, release the stress of the day, and prepare for restful sleep. Meditation before bed improves sleep quality, which helps to generate more of melatonin hormone which is thereby essential for DHT hormonal balance and hair health.

6.4.2 Overcoming Challenges

Dealing with Distractions: It's common to face distractions during meditation, especially when first starting. When distractions arise, gently bring your focus back to your breath or mantra without judgment. Over time, you'll find it easier to maintain focus and enter a deeper meditative states.

Staying Consistent: Consistency is key to reaping the full benefits of Raj Yoga meditation. If you miss a session, don't get discouraged. Simply return to your practice the next day. Setting a specific time for meditation each day can help you stay committed to your routine.

Managing Time Constraints: If you have a busy schedule, start with shorter meditation sessions, gradually increasing the duration as you become more comfortable. Even 5-10 minutes of meditation can make a difference in your coping ability, stress levels and overall well-being.

6.4.3 Enhancing the Meditation Experience

Incorporating Aroma therapy: Essential oils such as lavender, sandalwood, or frankincense can enhance your meditation experience. Diffusing these oils in your meditation space or applying them to your wrists or temples can help create a calming atmosphere and deepen your relaxation.

Using Meditation Music: Soft, soothing music or nature sounds can help drown out external noises and support your meditation practice. Choose music that resonates with you and enhances your focus and relaxation.

Joining a Meditation Group: If you find it challenging to meditate on your own, consider joining a meditation group or class. Meditating with others can provide motivation, support, and a sense of community, making it easier to establish and maintain your practice.

6.5 Real-Life Applications and Success Stories

The transformative power of Raj Yoga meditation is evident in the experiences of those who have embraced the practice. This section highlights real-life success stories and provides practical tips for making Raj Yoga meditation a part of your daily routine.

6.5.1 Case Study: Overcoming Stress-Related Hair Loss

A 40-year-old man experienced significant hair loss due to chronic stress and anxiety. Despite trying various treatments, his hair continued to thin, leading to further stress and frustration. On the recommendation of the author, he began practicing Raj Yoga meditation for 20 minutes each morning and evening.

Within a few months, he noticed a reduction in his stress levels, improved sleep quality, and a gradual decrease in hair shedding. Over time, his hair began to regain its thickness and strength, and his overall well-being improved. Raj Yoga meditation not only helped him manage stress but also supported his journey to healthier hair.

6.5.2 Practical Tips for Success

Start Small: If you're new to meditation, begin with short sessions of 5-10 minutes and gradually increase the duration as you become more comfortable with the practice. The key is to start where you are and build from there.

Create a Ritual: Establish a ritual around your meditation practice, such as lighting a candle, playing soft music, or diffusing essential oils. These rituals can help signal to your mind that it's time to relax and focus inward.

Be Patient: Meditation is a practice that requires patience and persistence. Don't be discouraged if you don't see immediate results. With consistent practice, the benefits of Raj Yoga meditation will gradually unfold, leading to improved mental clarity, reduced stress, and healthier hair.

Conclusion

Raj Yoga meditation offers a powerful tool for enhancing hair health by addressing the mental and emotional factors that contribute to hair loss. By cultivating inner peace, reducing stress, and promoting hormonal balance, Raj Yoga meditation creates a holistic environment where hair can thrive. As you integrate this practice into your daily routine, remember that the journey to inner peace and healthy hair is a gradual process. With dedication and consistency, Raj Yoga meditation can transform not only your hair but also your overall well-being, connecting yourself to higher consciousness leading to a more balanced and fulfilling purposeful life.

In the next chapter, we will explore modern treatments for hair loss, including the latest advances in medical and nutritional therapies that complement the holistic approaches discussed so far.

CHAPTER SEVEN

MODERN TREATMENTS FOR HAIR LOSS

Hair loss is a common concern affecting millions of people worldwide. While traditional remedies and holistic approaches like yoga and meditation play an essential role in promoting hair health, modern science has provided us with advanced treatments that try to address the underlying causes of hair loss more directly and at a quicker time. This chapter explores the latest research and developments in hair loss treatments, offering a comprehensive overview of medical, nutritional, and technological interventions that can help restore hair growth and improve hair health.

7.1 Understanding the Causes of Hair Loss

Before delving into specific treatments, it's crucial to understand the various factors that contribute to hair loss. The reasons for hair loss have already been disced in chapter one. I would urge the readers to read chapter one once again before proceeding further for better understanding. Identifying the root cause of hair loss is the first step in determining the most effective treatment.

Causes of hair loss can either be Genetics and Epigenetics. Genetics are transferred from parents to the children. Genetic modification is beyond our scope right now. So, it's better to focus on the modifiable factors which can be worked upon. Epigenetics are the modifiable factors which express the genetics in our life. So, if you can control the epigenetics, you can even control the expression of genetics. With better lifestyle, stress management and better diet we can try to control the epigenetics. But there is an issue of consistency in following these things in our day-to-day life. Many patients complain that they don't get time to perform these rituals in morning. Hence there is need for modern medications to treat the hair loss and thinning effectively before it gets too late. Here I (Dermatologist) would be discussing the important treatment aspects of hair loss which really works if followed properly. But in today era of easy availability of internet and many social media experts, there is a lot of confusion about treatment options. Here I would urge the readers to consult an expert dermatologist for treatment modalities of their hair loss and do not jump on self-medications.

7.2 Medical Treatments for Hair Loss

Modern medical treatments for hair loss try to focus on addressing the underlying causes, stimulating hair growth, and maintain the hair health. These treatments include medications, surgical procedures, and innovative therapies that have shown promising results in clinical studies. It is strongly recommended to consult an expert dermatologist before considering the medical treatments of hair loss. This book is just to guide and not an advice or consult to start your hair loss treatment on your own. There is no medication in this world which doesn't have some side effects, and same applies to hair loss medications as well.

7.2.1 Medications used to control and treat hair loss

Minoxidil lotion: Minoxidil is a topical medication approved by the USA FDA for the treatment of Androgenetic alopecia. Its increases the blood supply to the hair follicles by various mechanisms. Now if the blood has good nutrition and good oxygen levels (available for the hair), it would be delivered to the hair roots. The roots will make good thick hair and also help in repair of the existing thin hair. Sometimes it is not possible to repair the existing hair, so the roots start making a new hair and pushes the thin hair outside. As a result, there is some amount of hair loss even for 2-3 months after starting minoxidil lotions. It is recommended to continue minoxidil lotion for atleast 6 months to 1 year to get optimal results. It works by stimulating hair follicles and prolonging the anagen phase of the hair cycle. Minoxidil is available over-the-counter in 2% and 5% formulations and is applied directly to the scalp. Studies have shown that minoxidil can promote hair regrowth in both men and women, though results may vary, and continued use is necessary to maintain hair growth. Many patients are reluctant to start minoxidil because they have heard and read on internet that once you start minoxidil, you cannot stop. But this is just a myth. The work of minoxidil is to increase the blood flow. This can actually be done by consistent yoga poses and meditation which has already been discussed in detail in previous chapters. So, if you start practicing the yoga and meditation consistently for a longer time, you can stop application of minoxidil.

Minoxidil tablets: Low Dose Oral Minoxidil (LDOM) is the latest form of minoxidil after lotions. Around 75 to 80% of patients of hair loss discontinue using minoxidil lotion because of various reasons. Itching, redness, dandruff, allergies are the prominent reasons for the noncompliance. And hence they shift to Ecom available products which are well marketed, costly and which may not be that effective. I give oral minoxidil tablets in low doses to my patients and gets wonderful results. You must consult an expert dermatologist if you consider oral minoxidil as a form of hair loss treatment.

Finasteride: We have read in chapter 1 about the stress hormone DHT, which causes hair loss. So, we need some medications which can control the action of this hormone to control hair loss. Even though we know that Raj Yoga and stress management can control this stress hormone, we are reluctant to do it consistently. Also, certain food like tomatoes, carrots, pumpkin seeds etc have the ability to control DHT, we don't consume adequate amount in our diet. As a result, there is a need for DHT blocker medications. Finasteride is an oral medication (USA FDA approved that inhibits the enzyme 5-alpha-reductase, which converts testosterone to DHT. By reducing DHT levels, finasteride helps prevent hair follicle miniaturization and slows the progression of Androgenetic alopecia. Finasteride is more commonly prescribed for men, as it can cause birth defects if used by women of childbearing age. Studies have shown that finasteride is effective in reducing hair loss and promoting hair regrowth in men, with long-term use leading to significant improvements.

Dutasteride: This molecule is the big brother of finasteride and works slightly better. It is FDA Japan, South Korea and Taiwan approved for treating Androgenetic alopecia hair loss. I have been managing many patients of Androgenetic alopecia with dutasteride with fantastic results. As per scientific studies the side effect profile is slightly better or same as of finasteride.

Melatonin: As we have discussed in chapter 1 about the importance of melatonin in maintaining healthy hair growth and thickness. Also, adequate melatonin levels in body helps in controlling DHT action of hair loss. Melatonin is of utmost importance for having healthy hair. Lack of adequate timely sleep, lack of morning sun light exposure reduces the secretion of melatonin in the body. Hence it becomes mandatory for patients to sleep on time and have adequate quality sleep to treat their hair loss. But there are many patients who are unable to sleep even if they go on bed on time. So, for such patients, melatonin tablets can be of great help. Melatonin will induce timely good quality sleep in patients of hair loss, reduce activity of DHT at the hair follicle, also calms the brain cells and increase the coping ability to tackle stress. These actions then help the hair to grow stronger and healthier. I have been giving melatonin to my patients of hair loss with good success.

Cyclical Nutritional Therapy: This has been discussed in chapter one, very important aspects of reduced nutritional levels of our food, the difference between traditional farming and modern-day farming. Also, it has been discussed how the society today is overfed yet malnourished of nutritional elements. As a result, the I feel that we are in a state of subclinical deficiency of nutritional elements and suggest to take good nutritional supplements to compensate for the deficiency. Now it's time to understand once again as to why it's better to have cyclical nutritional supplement than daily dosages of nutrition. Some nutritional elements are friends of each other, so it's advisable to take them together to help in absorption and metabolism. A good example of this is Iron, if taken along with vitamin C and vitamin A helps in absorption and better utilisation by the body. Calcium when taken with vitamin D3 helps each other with better absorption, and metabolism. On the other hand, there are some nutritional elements which are not so good friends of each other. It's advisable to not take them together. A good example of this is Iron and Calcium if taken together inhibits absorption and utilization of each other.

Having said that there are studies which shows that nutrients if taken on consecutive and alternate days give better results than taking it every day. Iron supplement if taken alternate days has better absorption and utilization by body rather than daily intake.

By cycling the nutrients, the body has time to absorb and use them effectively, reducing the risk of toxicity or reduced absorption due to nutrient competition.

There is one another cyclical requirement of hair follicle. It is based on the understanding that different nutrients are needed at different times during the hair growth cycle. But this is not practiced so routinely.

7.2.2 Platelet-Rich Plasma (PRP) Therapy:

There are few selected patients who do not respond even after 6 months of medications and who fail to follow the other aspects like meditation, yoga and diet. For such patients it becomes important to give some interventional management. Platelet rich plasma (PRP) is one of the safer and effective means for such kind of patients.

How PRP Works: PRP therapy involves drawing a small amount of the patient's blood, processing it to concentrate the platelets with its activated growth factors, and then injecting the platelet-rich plasma into the scalp. Platelets with their growth factors stimulate hair follicles, promote healing, and encourage hair growth. PRP therapy is often used in conjunction with other treatments, such as minoxidil or finasteride, to enhance results.

Efficacy of PRP: Clinical studies and my own personal experience have shown that PRP therapy can improve hair density, increase hair thickness, and reduce hair shedding in individuals with Androgenetic alopecia and other types of hair loss. While PRP therapy is generally safe and well-tolerated, multiple sessions are usually required to achieve optimal results, and maintenance treatments may be necessary.

7.2.3 iPRF therapy:

iPRF (injectable Platelet Rich Fibrin) therapy is an advanced, third generation PRP, natural treatment for hair loss, known for its regenerative properties. It involves the use of a patient's own blood, processed to concentrate fibrin and platelets, which are then injected into the scalp to stimulate hair growth. It is very effective in those experiencing early thinning or mild to moderate hair loss and can be used in patients after a hair transplant to support healing and enhance hair growth. Typically, 5-6 sessions are recommended, spaced 4-6 weeks apart, for optimal results.

How iPRF Therapy Works: A small amount of the patient's blood is drawn, usually from the arm. The blood is then spun at a lower speed (compared to PRP) to separate the platelet-rich fibrin, which contains growth factors, stem cells, and white blood cells. The fibrin is injected into areas of the scalp experiencing hair thinning or loss. The growth factors in iPRF promote healing and stimulate the hair follicles, potentially increasing the density and thickness of hair. Unlike PRP therapy, iPRF releases growth factors over a longer period, providing sustained support for hair follicle health.

Key Benefits of iPRF for Hair Loss:

Natural Approach: Since the treatment uses your body's own blood components, there are no external chemicals, there's minimal risk of allergic reactions or side effects.
Longer Release of Growth Factors: iPRF releases growth factors over time, leading to prolonged stimulation of the hair follicles.
Enhanced Hair Follicle Regeneration: iPRF can enhance hair density by encouraging follicle regeneration and reducing hair shedding.

iPRF vs. PRP (Platelet-Rich Plasma) Therapy:

Fibrin vs. Plasma: PRP uses plasma rich in platelets, while iPRF uses fibrin, which forms a scaffold that holds platelets in place, allowing a slower, more prolonged release of growth factors.
Cellular Content: iPRF contains more concentrated platelets, stem cells, and white blood cells, which may enhance its regenerative properties.

Longevity: The release of growth factors in iPRF is longer than PRP, potentially offering more sustained benefits for hair growth.

Combining iPRF with Other Therapies:

iPRF can be combined with other treatments, such as:
Minoxidil or Finasteride: For enhanced results when treating Androgenetic alopecia.
Microneedling: To improve scalp absorption of growth factors.
Low-Level Laser Therapy (LLLT): A complementary treatment that further stimulates hair follicles.

7.2.4 Low-Level Laser Therapy (LLLT)

Mechanism of Action: Low-level laser therapy (LLLT) involves using low-intensity lasers or light-emitting diodes (LEDs) to stimulate hair follicles and promote hair growth. The light energy penetrates the scalp and increases cellular activity, improving blood flow to hair follicles and prolongs the anagen phase of the hair cycle.

Effectiveness of LLLT: LLLT devices, such as laser combs, helmets, and caps, are available for home use and have been shown to be effective in treating Androgenetic alopecia. Clinical studies have demonstrated that LLLT can increase hair density, improve hair thickness, and slow the progression of hair loss. LLLT is most effective when used consistently over several months, and results may vary depending on the severity of hair loss.

7.2.5 Microneedling

How Microneedling Works: Microneedling involves creating tiny micro-injuries in the scalp using a device with fine needles. These micro-injuries stimulate the body's natural healing response, leading to increased production of collagen and growth factors that promote hair growth. Microneedling is often combined with other treatments, such as PRP, iPRF or topical minoxidil, growth stimulators, protein peptides to enhance results.

Effectiveness of Microneedling: Clinical studies have shown that microneedling can improve hair density and thickness in individuals with Androgenetic alopecia. It is a minimally invasive procedure with a low risk of side effects, making it a popular option for those seeking non-surgical hair restoration. Ideally performed once a month and for 6-8 months duration.

7.2.6 Hair Transplant Surgery:

Hair transplant is a surgical option for the patients who are into late stages of hair loss. In such cases the roots of the hair follicles in front area are dead. No medicines or procedures would work to regrow new hair. Hence, we would need to transfer hair follicles with the roots from the back side of the head (occipital area with good hair) to the front side. I would recommend hair transplant surgery only when all the medical options fail to stop hair loss and increase hair volume.

Types of Hair Transplants: Hair transplant surgery is a surgical solution for hair loss that involves moving hair follicles from a donor area (typically the back or sides of the scalp) to a balding or thinning area. The two main types of hair transplant procedures are follicular unit transplantation (FUT) and follicular unit extraction (FUE).

FUT: In FUT, a strip of scalp is removed from the donor area, and individual hair follicles are extracted and transplanted to the recipient area. FUT can transplant a large number of follicles in a single session but may leave a linear scar at the donor site which is not acceptable to many patients. There is a longer recovery downtime after the surgery.

FUE: In FUE, which is a newer technology, individual hair follicles are extracted directly from the donor area using a specialized tool and then transplanted to the recipient area. FUE leaves minimal scarring and has a shorter recovery time. I have been performing FUE hair transplant for more than 15 years now. It is quite safe and effective means to restore the lost hair and lost confidence of the patient.

Success Rates and Considerations: Hair transplant surgery has a high success rate, with most patients experiencing significant improvement in hair density and coverage. However, the outcome depends on factors such as the skill of the surgeon, the quality of the donor hair, and the patient's adherence to post-operative care. Hair transplants are typically recommended for individuals with stable hair loss who have sufficient donor hair. It takes about 9 months to a year to get good results after the surgery.

7.2.7 Scalp Micropigmentation (SMP)

What is SMP: Scalp Micropigmentation (SMP) is a non-surgical cosmetic procedure that involves tattooing tiny dots on the scalp to create the appearance of hair follicles. SMP is used to simulate the look of a closely-shaven scalp or to add density to thinning areas.

Advantages and Limitations: SMP is a suitable option for individuals who are not candidates for hair transplant surgery or who want a low-maintenance solution for hair loss or who are scared of surgery. While SMP does not restore hair growth, it can effectively camouflage bald spots and create the illusion of fuller hair. The results of SMP are semi-permanent, with touch-ups required every few years.

7.3 Advanced and Emerging Hair Loss Treatments

As research continues to advance, new and innovative treatments for hair loss are emerging. These cutting-edge therapies offer promising results for individuals who have not responded to traditional treatments or who are seeking additional options to enhance hair growth.

7.3.1 Stem Cell Therapy

How Stem Cells Work: Stem cells have the unique ability to develop into various types of cells, including hair follicle cells. Stem cell therapy for hair loss involves harvesting stem cells from the patient's own body (usually from adipose tissue or bone marrow), processing them, and then injecting them into the scalp. These stem cells stimulate hair follicle regeneration and promote hair growth.

Research and Results: Early studies on stem cell therapy for hair loss have shown promising results, with patients experiencing increased hair density and thickness. However, stem cell therapy is still in the experimental stages, and more research is needed to determine its long-term efficacy and safety.

7.3.2 Exosome Therapy

What are Exosomes: Exosomes are small vesicles that are released by cells and contain proteins, lipids, and RNA. They play a role in cell-to-cell communication and can influence the behavior of surrounding cells. In hair loss treatment, exosomes are used to deliver growth factors and signaling molecules to hair follicles, promoting regeneration and growth.

Clinical Potential: Exosome therapy is an emerging treatment that has shown potential in early studies. It is believed to be more potent than PRP therapy due to the concentrated delivery of growth factors. However, like stem cell therapy, exosome therapy is still in the experimental phase, and further research is required to establish its effectiveness.

7.4 Combining Treatments for Optimal Results

While individual treatments can be effective, combining multiple therapies often yields the best results. A multi-faceted approach that addresses the various causes of hair loss can enhance hair regrowth and improve overall hair health.

7.4.1 Combining Medical, Cyclical Nutritional and Interventional Treatments

Minoxidil and Cyclical Nutritional Therapy: Combining topical minoxidil or oral minoxidil with cyclical nutritional supplements like Hair Fact or Gro-Hint can support hair regrowth from both the inside and outside. Minoxidil increases blood flow which helps in delivering the nutritional supplements to the hair follicles and stimulates hair follicles to support healthy hair growth. This works good for both male and female with hair loss and hair thinning.

Minoxidil, Cyclical Nutritional and Finasteride: For men with Androgenetic alopecia, combining finasteride with minoxidil and cyclical nutritional therapy will not only help reduce DHT levels but increase the blood supply to hair which will help in delivering the nutritional supplements to the hair follicles and stimulates hair follicles to support healthy hair growth. This combination works on bimodal action, reduces hair loss by blocking DHT and improves hair growth by increasing blood supply and nutrition.

Minoxidil, Cyclical Nutritional, Finasteride and iPRF Therapy: For men with Androgenetic alopecia, combining finasteride with minoxidil and cyclical nutritional therapy and iPRF therapy with be of greater success. It can help reduce DHT levels, reduce hair loss and; increase the blood supply to hair which helps in delivering the nutritional supplements to the hair follicles and stimulates hair follicles to support healthy hair growth. Also, the iPRF in this combination will help in regenerative aspects of hair loss, providing a comprehensive treatment approach.

Minoxidil, Cyclical Nutritional and iPRF Therapy: For men and women with hair loss and hair thinning minoxidil and cyclical nutritional therapy and iPRF therapy will be of greater advantage. It can increase the blood supply to hair which helps in delivering the nutritional supplements to the hair follicles and stimulates hair follicles to support healthy hair growth. Also, the iPRF in this combination will help in regenerative aspects of hair loss, providing a comprehensive treatment approach.

iPRF and Microneedling: Combining iPRF therapy with microneedling can enhance the effects of both treatments. Microneedling increases the action of iPRF in the scalp tissue, leading to more significant improvements in hair density and thickness. This option is for someone who doesn't want to take medicines on daily basis. However, this option is less effective when done in isolation without oral medications.

Stem Cell Therapy and Exosome Therapy: For individuals seeking cutting-edge treatments, combining stem cell therapy with exosome therapy may offer enhanced regenerative effects. This combination targets hair follicle regeneration at multiple levels, promoting stronger and healthier hair growth. However, this is still in experimental stages and will take more time to get adequate data about its results potentials and safety.

7.5 Monitoring Progress and Adjusting Treatment

Hair loss treatments require time and patience to show results. It's important to monitor progress and adjust treatments as needed to achieve the best possible outcome.

7.5.1 Tracking Progress

Photographic Documentation: Taking regular photographs of your scalp can help you track progress and assess the effectiveness of your treatment. Photos should be taken under consistent lighting and from multiple angles to provide a clear comparison over time.

Trichoscopy and Hair Density Measurements: My clinic offers computerized analysis which shows the condition of scalp surface, hair diameter diversity (HDD), hair shaft abnormality and hair density measurements. These measurements can provide objective data on the effectiveness of your treatment.

7.5.2 Adjusting Treatment Plans

Evaluating Effectiveness: If you do not see noticeable improvements after several months of treatment, it may be necessary to adjust your treatment plan. This could involve increasing the dosage of the medication, adding a new therapy, or exploring alternative treatments as per experts' advice.

Consulting with a Specialist: Regular consultations with a dermatologist or hair loss specialist are essential for monitoring progress and making informed decisions about your treatment. A specialist can provide guidance on the most effective combination of treatments and help you navigate any challenges that arise during your treatment schedule.

7.6 Success Stories and Real-Life Applications

The following case studies illustrate how modern hair loss treatments have helped individuals achieve significant improvements in hair growth and overall hair health.

7.6.1 Case Study: Male Pattern Baldness Treated with Finasteride, low dose oral minoxidil, Cyclical Nutritional Therapy and iPRF therapy

Patient Profile: A 35-year-old man with a family history of male pattern baldness began noticing hair thinning in his early 30s. Concerned about his receding hairline and thinning crown, he consulted my clinic, was recommended a combination of oral finasteride, low dose oral minoxidil, Cyclical Nutritional kit and iPRF therapy.

Treatment and Results: After six months of treatment, the patient noticed a reduction in hair shedding and some regrowth in the thinning areas. Continued treatment over the next year led to significant improvements in hair density, with fuller coverage at the crown and a more defined hairline. The patient was pleased with the results and continued the combination therapy to maintain his progress.

7.6.2 Case Study: Female patient with Hair Thinning addressed with low dose oral Minoxidil and Cyclical Nutritional kit

Patient Profile: A 45-year-old woman experienced diffuse hair thinning across her scalp, likely due to a combination of hormonal changes and stress. She had tried various over-the-counter treatments with little success and sought professional advice.

Treatment and Results: The patient was prescribed low dose oral minoxidil and recommended to take cyclical nutritional kit. After three months, she noticed less hair shedding and improved hair thickness. Over the course of a year, her hair became noticeably fuller, and she regained confidence in her appearance.

7.6.3 Case Study: Cyclical Nutritional kit, iPRF therapy and Microneedling for Alopecia Areata

Patient Profile: A 28-year-old woman was diagnosed with Alopecia areata, resulting in patchy hair loss on her scalp. She was concerned about the progression of the condition and wanted to explore treatment options.

Treatment and Results: The patient was prescribed cyclical nutritional kit and underwent a series of iPRF treatments combined with microneedling. After several sessions, she saw thick hair growth in the affected areas, and the patches began to fill in. Continued treatment helped stabilize her condition and promote further regrowth.

Conclusion

Modern treatments for hair loss offer a wide range of options, from medications and supplements to advanced therapies like iPRF, PRP, Microneedling and Scalp Micro-pigmentation. By understanding the underlying causes of hair loss and selecting the appropriate combination of treatments, individuals can achieve significant improvements in hair growth and overall hair health. While each treatment has its strengths and limitations, the key to success lies in a personalized, multi-faceted approach that addresses the unique needs of each individual.

As you continue your journey to healthier hair, remember that patience and consistency are essential elements. Hair growth is a gradual process, and it may take several months to see noticeable results. By combining modern treatments with healthy lifestyle choices and stress management techniques, you can create the optimal conditions for your hair to thrive. Here once again its important to remind that an expert dermatologist's consult is required to start these medical options.

In the next chapter, we will explore the importance of scalp care and how it plays a crucial role in supporting healthy hair growth. Proper scalp care routines, effective shampoos, and topical treatments will be discussed to help you maintain a healthy environment for your hair follicles.

CHAPTER EIGHT

Scalp Care Essentials

The health of your scalp is fundamental in maintaining strong, vibrant hair. Often overlooked, the scalp plays a crucial role in hair growth, as it provides the foundation for healthy follicles. Just as soil quality affects the growth of plants, the condition of your scalp can either support or hinder hair health. This chapter delves into the essential aspects of scalp care, exploring the science behind it, key practices for maintaining a healthy scalp, and effective products like shampoos, serums, and treatments to promote hair vitality.

8.1 Why Scalp Health Matters

Healthy hair starts with a healthy scalp. A well-nourished, clean, and balanced scalp creates an optimal environment for hair follicles to function effectively. Just like we have gut microbiome, we also have a scalp microbiome. Scalp microbiome is an apt combination of natural oils and good friendly microorganisms (bacteria and fungus) residing on the scalp around the hair follicles. If there is any alteration in the composition of these microorganisms, it leads to unhealthy scalp condition. When scalp conditions are neglected and become unhealthy, it can lead to a variety of issues such as dryness, dandruff, inflammation, or clogged follicles - all of which can contribute to hair loss and hair thinning. Its very important to establish and maintain the right composition of scalp microbiome for healthy shiny hair.

8.1.1 Scalp Anatomy and Hair Growth

Hair Follicles: Hair follicles are tiny structures embedded in the scalp that are responsible for hair growth. Each follicle goes through a cycle of growth (anagen), rest (telogen), and shedding (catagen). Healthy follicles are necessary for robust hair growth.

Sebaceous Glands: These glands are attached to the hair follicles and secrete sebum, a natural oil that moisturizes the scalp and hair. Sebum keeps the scalp hydrated and helps protect the skin barrier. However, imbalances in sebum production - either too much or too little - can lead to scalp issues like oiliness, dandruff, or dryness, all of which can impair hair health. This imbalance can be caused due to improper diet, bad lifestyle like sleeping late , high screen time late evenings and night. This imbalance of natural oil production alters the scalp microbiome which damages the hair follicle and retards its growth.

Blood Circulation: The scalp has a rich network of blood vessels that supply oxygen and nutrients to hair follicles. Poor circulation can starve follicles of these essential nutrients, leading to weakened hair and increased shedding.

8.1.2 Common Scalp Issues That Affect Hair Health

Dry Scalp: A dry scalp is often characterized by flakiness, tightness, and itching. This condition can lead to weakened hair follicles and increased breakage. Common causes include cold weather, harsh hair products, or frequent washing with hot water, hormonal imbalance like hypothyroid.

Oily Scalp: Excessive sebum production leads to an oily scalp, which can clog pores, trap dirt, and create an environment for fungal growth. Oily scalps often suffer from conditions like seborrheic dermatitis (dandruff), which can cause irritation and hair thinning. Fried and junk food is also known to give oily scalp.

Inflammation: Scalp inflammation, caused by conditions like psoriasis, eczema, or allergic reactions, cigarette smoking, pollution of the city, disrupts the hair growth cycle. Chronic inflammation can lead to hair thinning or permanent follicle damage.

Dandruff: Dandruff is a common scalp condition marked by flaking and itching, typically caused by an overgrowth of a yeast called Malassezia. While dandruff doesn't directly cause hair loss, excessive scratching and irritation can damage hair follicles and lead to hair thinning.

8.2 The Importance of a Scalp Care Routine

Developing a consistent scalp care routine is essential for maintaining a healthy environment of scalp microbiome which will in turn give healthy hair growth. Just as you would care for your skin with a regular cleansing, moisturizing, and treatment regimen, your scalp requires similar attention.

8.2.1 Cleansing the Scalp

Shampoo Frequency: How often you should wash your hair depends on your scalp type- whether it is oily, dry, or balanced. Overwashing can strip the scalp of natural oils and friendly microorganisms (scalp microbiome), leading to dryness and irritation, while under-washing can allow product buildup and excess oil to clog follicles. For most people, washing two to three times a week is ideal.

Choosing the Right Shampoo: Selecting a shampoo that matches your scalp type is crucial. For oily scalps, look for clarifying shampoos that remove excess oil without over-drying. For dry or sensitive scalps, opt for gentle, moisturizing shampoos free from harsh sulfates or parabens.

Sulfate-Free Shampoos: Sulfates are common ingredients in shampoos that create lather, but they can be harsh and strip the scalp of its natural oils. Sulfate-free shampoos are gentler and help maintain the scalp's natural moisture balance.

Shampoos for Dandruff: For those dealing with dandruff or seborrheic dermatitis, medicated shampoos containing active ingredients like zinc pyrithione, ketoconazole, or selenium sulfide can help control flaking and fungal overgrowth.

Exfoliating the Scalp: Scalp exfoliation helps remove dead skin cells, product buildup, and excess sebum and establishes the scalp microbiome. It also stimulates circulation, encouraging healthy hair growth. Exfoliating shampoos or scrubs, typically containing salicylic acid or gentle exfoliants, can be used once a week.

8.2.2 Moisturizing and Nourishing the Scalp

Conditioners and Leave-In Treatments: After cleansing, it's essential to follow up with a conditioner to restore moisture to the scalp and hair. Conditioners help seal the cuticles on the surface of hair and prevent dryness. For those with dry or sensitive scalps, leave-in conditioners or scalp serums that provide long-lasting hydration can be beneficial.

Scalp Oils and Serums: Scalp oils and serums containing nourishing ingredients like tea tree oil, peppermint oil, or argan oil can help maintain moisture balance and soothe irritation. Oils like jojoba and coconut oil mimic the scalp's natural sebum and provide deep hydration without clogging pores.

DIY Scalp Treatments: Homemade scalp treatments using natural ingredients like aloe vera, honey, or avocado can provide additional nourishment and hydration. Aloe vera, for example, has anti-inflammatory properties that can soothe irritation, while honey acts as a humectant, attracting moisture to the scalp.

8.2.3 Stimulating the Scalp

Scalp Massage: Regular scalp massage improves blood circulation, which helps deliver oxygen and nutrients to hair follicles. It also helps distribute natural oils across the scalp, preventing dryness and promoting a healthier environment for hair growth. Scalp massage can be done with your fingers or with a specialized scalp massager.

Techniques : Massage your scalp using circular motions with gentle pressure. Focus on areas where you experience tension or where hair seems thinner. A daily 5-minute scalp massage can significantly boost circulation and stimulate hair growth over time.

Inversion Therapy: Inversion therapy or Sirsasana involves hanging your head upside down for short periods to increase blood flow to the scalp. While evidence on its effectiveness is limited, some people find that combining inversion with scalp massage enhances the benefits of both practices. Preferably done under expert guidance.

8.3 Scalp Treatments for Specific Conditions

If you suffer from specific scalp conditions like dandruff, inflammation, or hair thinning, targeted treatments by an expert dermatologist can help address the underlying issues while promoting healthier hair growth.

8.3.1 Dandruff Treatments

Medicated Shampoos: As mentioned earlier, shampoos containing zinc pyrithione, ketoconazole, or selenium sulfide are effective in controlling dandruff. These antifungal ingredients help reduce the overgrowth of Malassezia yeast, which is often responsible for dandruff. For mild cases, over-the-counter options may be sufficient, but more severe cases may require prescription-strength formulations.

Tea Tree Oil: Tea tree oil has natural antifungal and anti-inflammatory properties, making it a popular choice for treating dandruff and other scalp irritations. Look for shampoos or scalp treatments containing tea tree oil, or add a few drops of tea tree oil to your regular shampoo for an extra boost.

8.3.2 Scalp Psoriasis and Eczema

Corticosteroid Treatments: For individuals with scalp psoriasis or eczema, topical corticosteroids can help reduce inflammation and itching. These medications come in various forms, including shampoos, creams, and foams, and are often prescribed by dermatologists to manage flare-ups.

Coal Tar Shampoos: Coal tar shampoos help slow the overproduction of skin cells, which is a hallmark of psoriasis. While effective, these shampoos have a strong odor and can stain clothing, so they should be used with care.

8.3.3 Seborrheic Dermatitis

Ketoconazole Shampoos: Ketoconazole is an antifungal agent effective in treating seborrheic dermatitis. It reduces the yeast population on the scalp and controls inflammation and flaking. Shampoos containing ketoconazole are often used 2-3 times per week to maintain scalp health.

Salicylic Acid: Salicylic acid helps exfoliate the scalp, removing excess skin cells and reducing scaling. It is often included in treatments for both dandruff and seborrheic dermatitis, as it helps prevent clogged follicles and buildup.

8.4 Choosing the Right Products for Scalp Health

With so many products in the market, choosing the right ones for your scalp can be overwhelming. However, understanding the key ingredients to look for and how they benefit your scalp can simplify the process.

8.4.1 Key Ingredients for a Healthy Scalp

Zinc Pyrithione: Known for its antifungal and antibacterial properties, zinc pyrithione is commonly used in dandruff shampoos to reduce flaking and control fungal growth on the scalp.

Salicylic Acid: This beta hydroxy acid (BHA) exfoliates dead skin cells and prevents buildup. It's beneficial for oily scalps and those suffering from dandruff or seborrheic dermatitis.

Ketoconazole: Ketoconazole is an antifungal agent effective against dandruff and seborrheic dermatitis. It helps reduce inflammation and yeast overgrowth on the scalp.

Tea Tree Oil: This natural essential oil has antimicrobial and anti-inflammatory properties, making it a great ingredient for treating dandruff, inflammation, and oily scalp conditions.

Peppermint Oil: Peppermint oil is known for its cooling and soothing properties. It can help improve blood circulation to the scalp and relieve itching and irritation.

Aloe Vera: Aloe vera is a natural moisturizer that soothes the scalp and reduces inflammation. It is especially beneficial for individuals with sensitive or dry scalps.

8.4.2 Avoiding Harmful Ingredients

Sulfates: Sulfates are harsh detergents found in many shampoos and cleansers. While they create a rich lather, they can strip the scalp of natural oils, leading to dryness and irritation. Opt for sulfate-free shampoos that are gentler on the scalp.

Parabens: Parabens are preservatives used in cosmetics, but they have been linked to potential health risks and can cause scalp irritation in some individuals. Look for paraben-free products, especially if you have sensitive skin.

Silicones: Silicones are used in hair products to add shine and smoothness, but they can build up on the scalp and clog hair follicles over time. Avoid products with heavy silicones, especially if you have an oily scalp.

8.5 DIY Scalp Treatments

Natural, at-home scalp treatments can be an effective and affordable way to improve scalp health and nourish your hair. Many common kitchen ingredients have properties that can soothe, moisturize, and cleanse the scalp.

8.5.1 DIY Scalp Scrub

Ingredients:

2 tablespoons of brown sugar
2 tablespoons of coconut oil
1 tablespoon of honey
A few drops of tea tree oil

Instructions :

Mix the ingredients in a small bowl to form a paste.

Apply the scrub to your scalp in the shower, gently massaging it in circular motions to exfoliate dead skin cells and remove buildup.

Rinse thoroughly and follow up with your regular shampoo and conditioner.

Use this scrub once a week to maintain a clean and healthy scalp.

8.5.2 DIY Aloe Vera Scalp Treatment

Ingredients:

2 tablespoons of aloe vera gel (fresh or store-bought)

1 tablespoon of coconut oil or jojoba oil

Instructions :

Combine the aloe vera gel and oil in a bowl.

Apply the mixture to your scalp, massaging it in to soothe irritation and moisturize the skin.

Leave the treatment on for 20-30 minutes before rinsing out with a gentle shampoo.

Repeat this treatment once a week to keep your scalp hydrated and healthy.

8.5.3 DIY Apple Cider Vinegar Rinse

Ingredients:

2 tablespoons of apple cider vinegar

1 cup of water

Instructions :

Mix the apple cider vinegar and water in a spray bottle.

After shampooing, spray the mixture onto your scalp and hair.

Let it sit for a few minutes before rinsing thoroughly with water.

Apple cider vinegar helps balance the scalp's pH levels and removes buildup, leaving your scalp refreshed.

8.6 Professional Scalp Treatments

For more severe scalp issues or if you're looking for a deeper cleanse, professional scalp treatments offered by dermatologists or salons can provide targeted care.

8.6.1 Scalp Detox Treatments

What is Scalp Detoxing: Scalp detox treatments are designed to deep-clean the scalp, removing product buildup, excess oil, and dead skin cells. These treatments often involve the use of exfoliating scrubs, steam treatments, and stimulating massage to improve scalp health and hair growth.

When to Consider a Scalp Detox: If you regularly use styling products, dry shampoo, or have oily hair, a scalp detox treatment can help reset the scalp, leaving it clean and refreshed. It is particularly beneficial for individuals with scalp conditions like dandruff, seborrheic dermatitis, or folliculitis.

8.6.2 Scalp Microneedling

How Microneedling Works: Scalp microneedling involves using a device with fine needles to create micro-injuries in the scalp. These tiny punctures stimulate the body's natural healing response, promoting the production of collagen and improving blood circulation. Microneedling can also enhance the absorption of topical treatments, such as minoxidil hair boosters or hair serums.

Benefits for Hair Growth: Studies have shown that microneedling can promote scalp microbiome, regulate the natural oil on scalp, soothens the scalp surface and promotes hair growth, particularly in individuals with Androgenetic alopecia and dry itchy scalp. It can also be used in combination with other treatments, such as PRP, iPRF therapy, to boost results.

8.7 Real-Life Success Stories and Tips for Scalp Health

Understanding the importance of scalp health is just the first step. Applying the right practices and using the correct products can lead to significant improvements in both scalp and hair health. Let's look at some real-life applications and success stories.

8.7.1 Case Study: Oily Scalp and Hair Thinning

The Problem: A 30-year-old woman struggled with an oily scalp and thinning hair, especially around her temples. Despite washing her hair daily, it remained greasy by the end of the day.

The Solution: She was advised by me to switch to a sulfate-free clarifying shampoo and reduced her washing frequency to three times a week. She also began using a scalp scrub once a week to remove excess oil and buildup. After incorporating regular scalp massages with tea tree oil, she noticed less greasiness and improved hair growth in the thinning areas.

Results: After four months of consistent care, her hair was noticeably fuller, and her scalp felt cleaner and less oily. She continued her new routine and maintained her results.

8.7.2 Practical Tips for Maintaining a Healthy Scalp

Be Consistent: Like any skincare routine, consistency is key to maintaining scalp health. Regular cleansing, exfoliating, and moisturizing will keep your scalp in optimal condition.

Listen to Your Scalp: Pay attention to how your scalp feels. If it's excessively dry or oily, adjust your routine or try new products to restore balance. Don't ignore signs of irritation or inflammation, as these can lead to more serious issues if left untreated. Don't just listen to your friends or work colleague regarding a certain online product. If something worked for her scalp doesn't mean it would work on ur scalp also.

Seek Professional Help When Needed: If you're dealing with persistent scalp issues like dandruff, psoriasis, or unexplained hair loss, consult a dermatologist. They can recommend treatments or medications that address the root cause of your condition.

Conclusion

Caring for your scalp and scalp microbiome is a crucial, yet often overlooked, part of maintaining healthy hair. By adopting a scalp care routine that includes proper cleansing, moisturizing, and stimulation, you can maintain an apt scalp microbiome and create an ideal environment for hair follicles to thrive. Whether you suffer from dryness, oiliness, dandruff, or other scalp conditions, addressing these issues through the right products and treatments can make a significant difference in the health and appearance of your hair.

As you move forward in your hair health journey, remember that consistency and attentiveness to your scalp's needs are key. In the next chapter, we'll explore how to create a personalized hair health plan, combining modern treatments, scalp care, and lifestyle changes for long-term hair vitality.

CHAPTER NINE

Creating a Personal Hair Health Plan

Achieving and maintaining healthy hair is a multi-faceted journey that requires a personalized approach. Just as no two individuals are alike, neither are their hair needs. Factors like genetics, lifestyle, diet, hormones, stress, pollution, cosmetics and hair care habits, and underlying medical conditions all influence hair health. In this chapter, we will walk through the steps of creating a personalized hair health plan that combines modern treatments, scalp care, nutrition, and holistic lifestyle changes. This plan will help you address specific hair concerns and promote long-term hair vitality.

9.1 Assessing Your Hair and Scalp Health

Before developing a hair health plan, it's essential to assess your current hair and scalp condition. Understanding the state of your hair, scalp, and any underlying issues will help you tailor a plan that addresses your specific needs. Its important to seek an expert advice by an expert dermatologist regarding the assessment and creating a plan.

9.1.1 Identifying Hair Type

Straight, Wavy, Curly, or Coily: Your hair type plays a significant role in determining how it responds to different products and treatments. For example, straight hair tends to become oily more quickly, while curly and coily hair types often require more moisture to prevent dryness.

Fine, Medium, or Thick: The thickness of your individual hair strands also affects hair care choices. Fine hair is more prone to breakage and may need lighter products, while thick hair often requires heavier conditioning treatments to stay hydrated.

9.1.2 Understanding Scalp Type

Oily, Dry, or Balanced: Your scalp type determines how often you should cleanse your hair and what types of products to use. Oily scalps may benefit from more frequent washing with clarifying shampoos, while dry scalps need gentler, moisturizing cleansers to maintain balance.

Signs of Scalp Issues: Look for signs of scalp problems such as itching, flaking, redness, or irritation. Common issues like dandruff, seborrheic dermatitis, or psoriasis can all affect the health of your scalp and hair, and may require specific treatments.

9.1.3 Identifying Hair Concerns

Hair Loss or Thinning: If you are experiencing hair loss or thinning, identifying the underlying cause is key to choosing the right treatments. Hair loss can be due to factors like genetics, hormonal imbalances, stress, or nutritional deficiencies.

Breakage and Split Ends: Hair that is brittle or prone to breakage may be lacking in moisture or protein. Overprocessing from heat styling, chemical treatments, or coloring can exacerbate this problem. Hypothyroid is one of the commonest medical cause for dry hair and breakage.

Frizz and Dryness: Curly, wavy, and coily hair types are especially prone to frizz and dryness due to their structure. Environmental factors like humidity, sun exposure, and harsh weather conditions can also contribute to this issue.

9.2 Setting Realistic Hair Goals

Once you've assessed your current hair and scalp condition, the next step is to set realistic hair goals. Whether your aim is to grow thicker, stronger hair, prevent hair loss, or simply maintain healthy hair, having clear goals will help you stay focused on your hair health journey.

9.2.1 Defining Your Hair Goals

Hair Growth: If your primary goal is to increase hair length, focus on treatments and habits that promote the anagen (growth) phase of the hair cycle. This may include treatments like minoxidil, cyclical nutritional support, iPRF and scalp stimulation.

Improved Hair Density: For those looking to increase hair density, treatments that address hair loss, such as iPRF therapy, low-level laser therapy (LLLT), or cyclical nutritional supplements can be included in your plan.

Stronger, More Resilient Hair: If your hair is prone to breakage, you'll want to focus on deep conditioning treatments, protective styling, and products that help strengthen the hair shaft, such as protein treatments or bond-repairing products like Olaplex.

Healthier Scalp: Addressing scalp issues like dandruff, dryness, or excess oil production should be a priority. Incorporating scalp treatments such as exfoliation, proper cleansing, and the use of targeted scalp serums can help restore balance.

9.2.2 Timeframe for Achieving Goals

Short-Term Goals (1-3 Months): Set achievable short-term goals, such as reducing hair shedding, improving scalp health, or seeing an initial increase in hair growth. Short-term goals help keep you motivated and provide measurable progress.

Long-Term Goals (6-12 Months): Long-term goals, such as achieving a specific hair length or noticeably thicker hair, take time. Hair grows at an average rate of about half an inch per month, so it's important to be patient and consistent with your plan.

9.3 Crafting a Customized Hair Care Routine

Your daily hair care routine is the foundation of your hair health plan. This routine should include cleansing, conditioning, moisturizing, and protecting your hair and scalp. The products and techniques you choose should align with your hair type, scalp needs, and overall hair goals.

9.3.1 Choosing the Right Products

Shampoos and Cleansers: Select a shampoo that matches your scalp type and addresses any specific scalp issues you may have. For oily scalps, use a clarifying shampoo once a week to remove excess oil and buildup. For dry or sensitive scalps, opt for sulfate-free, moisturizing shampoos.

Conditioners: Choose a conditioner that provides the right balance of moisture and nourishment without weighing down your hair. For fine or oily hair, a lightweight, volumizing conditioner may be best, while thicker or curly hair may require a richer, more hydrating formula.

Leave-In Conditioners and Serums: Leave-in treatments add an extra layer of protection and hydration, especially for those with dry, frizzy, or damaged hair. Look for products with ingredients like argan oil, jojoba oil, or shea butter for deep hydration.

Heat Protection: If you use heat styling tools, always apply a heat protectant to prevent damage. Heat protectants create a barrier between your hair and styling tools, reducing the risk of breakage and split ends.

9.3.2 Incorporating Scalp Care

Scalp Exfoliation: Regularly exfoliating your scalp helps remove dead skin cells, excess oil, and product buildup that can clog hair follicles. Use a gentle scalp scrub or exfoliating shampoo once a week.

Scalp Massages: Daily scalp massages stimulate blood flow to the scalp, helping to nourish hair follicles and promote growth. You can use your fingertips or a scalp massager to gently massage your scalp for 5-10 minutes a day.

Specialized Scalp Treatments: If you're dealing with scalp conditions like dandruff, psoriasis, or seborrheic dermatitis, incorporate medicated treatments into your routine with help of an expert dermatologist. Shampoos containing ketoconazole, salicylic acid, or zinc pyrithione can help control inflammation and flaking.

9.3.3 Weekly and Monthly Treatments

Deep Conditioning: Incorporate a deep conditioning treatment once a week to restore moisture and repair damage. Products with ingredients like keratin, proteins, or oils can help strengthen the hair shaft and improve elasticity.

Protein Treatments: If your hair is weak or prone to breakage, adding a protein treatment to your routine once a while can help reinforce the hair structure. Be cautious not to overuse protein treatments, as too much protein can lead to hair stiffness and breakage.

Hot Oil Treatments: Hot oil treatments are especially beneficial for dry or curly hair types. Oils such as coconut, olive, or argan oil are warmed and applied to the hair and scalp to lock in moisture and add shine.

9.4 Integrating Modern Hair Loss Treatments

For individuals dealing with hair thinning or hair loss, modern treatments can be a vital part of a comprehensive hair health plan. You must seek expert guidance by a dermatologist for medications like minoxidil (topical or oral tablet), finasteride, dutasteride, melatonin to advanced therapies like microneedling, LLLT and iPRF therapy.

9.6 Lifestyle Changes to Support Hair Health

In addition to proper hair care and nutrition, making certain lifestyle changes can help support your hair health journey.

9.6.1 Managing Stress

Stress and Hair Loss: Chronic stress can lead to conditions like Telogen effluvium, where hair follicles prematurely enter the resting phase, leading to increased shedding. Managing stress through practices like yoga, meditation, or deep breathing can help increase the coping ability which then reduce hair loss and promote healthy hair growth.

Raj Yoga Meditation: Raj Yoga meditation, as discussed in Chapter 6, is particularly effective in calming the mind, reducing stress, and promoting emotional balance, all of which support hair health.

9.6.2 Getting Enough Sleep

The Importance of Sleep: Your body repairs and regenerates tissues, including hair follicles, during sleep. Poor sleep quality or insufficient sleep can disrupt melatonin hormonal balance and slow down hair growth. Aim for 6-8 hours of quality sleep (Ideal time is 10PM to 4 AM) each night to produce more melatonin which supports overall health and hair vitality.

9.6.3 Reducing Heat and Chemical Damage

Limit Heat Styling: Excessive use of heat styling tools like blow dryers, straighteners, and curling irons can weaken the hair shaft and lead to breakage. Use heat styling sparingly, and always apply a heat protectant before using any hot tools.

Avoid Harsh Chemicals: Chemical treatments like perms, relaxers, and hair dyes can damage the hair cuticle and lead to breakage. Opt for gentler, ammonia-free hair coloring products, and avoid overlapping chemical treatments.

9.7 Tracking Your Progress and Adjusting Your Plan

Creating a hair health plan is not a one-size-fits-all approach, and it's important to track your progress and make adjustments as needed.

9.7.1 Keeping a Hair Journal

Documenting Your Routine: Keep a journal to track the products you're using, treatments you've tried, and any noticeable changes in your hair and scalp. This can help you identify what's working and what may need to be adjusted.

Taking Photos: Take photos of your hair at regular intervals, such as every 3-4 weeks, to document your progress. Visual evidence can be helpful in tracking hair growth and assessing the effectiveness of your treatments.

9.7.2 Adjusting Your Plan

Reassessing Your Goals: After 3-6 months, reassess your hair goals and evaluate your progress. If you're not seeing the desired results, consider adjusting your routine, trying new products, or consulting with an expert dermatologist or trichologist.

Consistency is Key: Remember that hair growth takes time, and it is important to remain consistent with your routine. Most treatments take several months to show significant results, so be patient and stick to your plan.

Conclusion

Creating a personalized hair health plan involves understanding your unique hair and scalp needs, setting realistic goals, and incorporating the right products, treatments, and lifestyle changes into your routine. By focusing on scalp care, modern treatments, nutrition, and stress management, you can support healthier, stronger hair and address specific concerns like hair loss or thinning. Tracking your progress and making adjustments along the way will help ensure long-term hair vitality and success on your hair health journey. Its highly advisable to take guidance from an expert dermatologist for assessment and management of scalp and hair.

In the next chapter, we will discuss strategies for maintaining long-term hair health, including preventive measures, ongoing treatments, and how to adjust your routine as your hair needs evolve over time.

CHAPTER TEN

MAINTAINING LONG-TERM HAIR HEALTH

Achieving healthy hair is not a one-time goal; it requires ongoing care and attention. As your hair health evolves, maintaining long-term results involves adjusting your routine, staying consistent with treatments, and addressing any new challenges that arise. This chapter will focus on strategies to sustain healthy hair over time, including preventive measures, ongoing treatments, and how to adapt your hair care routine as your needs change.

10.1 Understanding the Hair Growth Cycle

The hair growth cycle plays a key role in how we approach long-term hair care. To maintain healthy hair, it's important to understand this cycle once again and how different factors can affect it.

10.1.1 The Phases of Hair Growth

Anagen (Growth Phase): This is the active growth phase of the hair cycle, lasting between 2 to 7 years, depending on genetics and other factors. Healthy hair grows approximately half an inch per month during this phase.

Catagen (Transitional Phase): Lasting 2 to 3 weeks, this is the short phase where hair growth slows down, and the hair follicle shrinks.

Telogen (Resting Phase): During this 3 to 4 month phase, hair rests before falling out and new growth begins. Typically, 10-15% of hair is in this phase at any given time.

Exogen (Shedding Phase): In this phase, hair is released from the follicle and falls out. A certain amount of hair shedding (50-100 hairs per day) is normal.

Maintaining long-term hair health involves supporting the anagen phase and minimizing disruptions to the hair cycle caused by stress, nutritional deficiencies, and scalp issues.

10.2 Preventive Measures for Long-Term Hair Health

Taking proactive steps to protect your hair and prevent damage is essential for long-term hair health. This includes addressing environmental factors, minimizing chemical and heat damage, and choosing protective hairstyles.

10.2.1 Protecting Hair from Environmental Damage

Sun Exposure: Prolonged sun exposure can damage both the hair and scalp. UV rays can degrade the hair cuticle, leading to dryness, frizz, and color fading. UV light can stimulate the bad bacteria on scalp surface to produce chemicals which can damage the scalp and hair cuticle. This damage generally happens in summer season, and the hair fall starts after 2-3 months i.e in monsoons. Wear hats or scarves to shield your hair from the sun, and use hair products with UV protection if you spend a lot of time outdoors.

Pollution: Air pollution with carbon particles can accumulate on the scalp, causing irritation, inflammation and clogging hair follicles. Regular cleansing with a clarifying shampoo can help remove pollutants and maintain a healthy scalp environment.

Water Quality: Hard water, which is rich in minerals like calcium and magnesium, can leave residues on the hair, making it dry and difficult to manage. Installing a shower filter can help reduce the effects of hard water, and using chelating shampoos can remove mineral buildup.

10.2.2 Minimizing Heat and Chemical Damage

Heat Styling: Excessive use of hot tools like straighteners, curling irons, and blow dryers can weaken the hair shaft, leading to breakage and split ends. To minimize heat damage, use heat styling tools sparingly, keep the temperature setting low, and always apply a heat protectant before styling.

Chemical Treatments: Hair coloring, relaxing, and perming can cause significant damage if done frequently. To maintain healthy hair, limit chemical treatments to every 6-9 months and choose ammonia-free, gentle formulations. Deep conditioning treatments should be used regularly to replenish moisture lost during chemical processes.

10.2.3 Protective Hairstyles

Low-Manipulation Styles: Hairstyles that minimize tension on the scalp and hair follicles, such as loose braids, buns, or twists, are ideal for protecting hair from breakage. Avoid tight ponytails or buns that pull on the scalp, as they can cause traction alopecia over time.

Silk or Satin Accessories: Using silk or satin pillowcases, bonnets, or scrunchies helps reduce friction between your hair and fabric, preventing breakage and frizz, especially for those with curly or textured hair.

10.3 Consistency in Hair Care Routine

Consistency is key to maintain long-term hair health. Regular care and attention help address emerging issues before they lead to significant damage or hair loss. A well-structured routine that includes cleansing, moisturizing, conditioning, and scalp care is essential.

10.3.1 Regular Cleansing and Scalp Care

Shampooing Frequency: Finding the right balance in shampooing frequency is important. While over-washing can strip the scalp of its natural oils, under-washing can lead to buildup and clogged follicles. For most hair types, washing 2-3 times per week with a sulfate-free shampoo is optimal. Adjust your routine based on scalp oiliness, product use, and lifestyle factors.

Scalp Maintenance: Regular scalp exfoliation helps remove dead skin cells and buildup, which can clog follicles and inhibit hair growth. Weekly use of scalp scrubs or exfoliating shampoos keeps the scalp clean and promotes circulation. Daily scalp massages, as discussed in previous chapters, stimulate blood flow to the follicles and support healthy hair growth.

10.3.2 Conditioning and Moisturizing

Daily Conditioning: Conditioning after every wash helps seal the hair cuticle, lock in moisture, and reduce frizz. For added moisture, use a leave-in conditioner or serum, particularly for dry or curly hair types.

Deep Conditioning: Incorporating a deep conditioning treatment once a week helps restore lost moisture, repair damage, and strengthen hair. Look for deep conditioners with ingredients like keratin, proteins, or nourishing oils (e.g., argan, coconut, or jojoba).

Moisturizing Oils: For those with dry or brittle hair, incorporating a moisturizing oil into your routine can help prevent breakage. Lightweight oils like argan oil provide moisture without weighing hair down, while heavier oils like coconut or castor oil are ideal for sealing in hydration on thicker hair types.

10.4 Adjusting Your Hair Care Routine Over Time

As your hair grows and changes, so too should your hair care routine. Factors such as age, health conditions, hormonal changes, and seasonal variations may require adjustments in how you care for your hair.

10.4.1 Seasonal Adjustments

Winter: Cold weather and indoor heating can lead to dryness and static, making it essential to increase moisturizing treatments during the winter months. Humidifiers can help maintain moisture in the air, preventing your scalp and hair from becoming too dry.

Summer: In the summer, hair is exposed to more UV rays, humidity, and chlorine from swimming pools. Use lightweight, hydrating products, and consider incorporating a leave-in conditioner with UV protection. Rinse hair with clean water after swimming to prevent chlorine damage.

10.4.2 Adapting to Hormonal Changes

Pregnancy and Postpartum: During pregnancy, hormonal changes often lead to thicker, more lustrous hair due to increased estrogen levels. However, many women experience postpartum hair shedding as hormone levels normalize. Focus on gentle hair care practices, and avoid aggressive treatments or hairstyles during this period.

Menopause: As estrogen levels decline during menopause, hair may become thinner and drier. Adapting your routine to include more hydrating and strengthening treatments can help maintain hair health. Scalp care is particularly important during this time, as hormonal changes can affect scalp oil production and lead to scalp microbiome imbalances.

Hypothyroid: Thyroid hormone imbalance leads to dry frizzy, breakage hairs. Also, the scalp surface gets dry and itchy. It is important to use light weight argan oil-based hair serums to avoid breakage. Also, its required to use scalp serums to avoid dryness and itching.

10.4.3 Managing Health-Related Hair Changes

Medications: Certain medications, including those for blood pressure, depression, or chemotherapy, can cause hair thinning or loss. If you notice significant changes in your hair due to medications, consult expert dermatologist to discuss potential treatments or adjustments to your hair care routine.

Stress and Hair Health: Chronic stress is a known contributor to hair thinning and shedding. Managing stress by increasing coping ability through meditation, exercise, or other relaxation techniques is vital for both overall health and maintaining hair vitality.

10.5 Monitoring Hair Health Over Time

Regularly assessing your hair health is essential for catching early signs of damage or hair loss. Monitoring changes in your hair's texture, thickness, and overall condition can help you make informed decisions about your hair care routine.

10.5.1 Tracking Hair Growth and Density

Photo Documentation: Take regular photos of your hair and scalp to monitor changes in hair growth, density, and scalp condition. Comparing photos taken a few months apart can help you identify areas where progress is being made or where adjustments are needed.

Measuring Hair Growth: Track your hair growth by measuring a small section of hair from the scalp to the ends. On average, hair grows about half an inch per month, but factors like diet, stress, and hair care habits can influence this rate.

10.5.2 Assessing the Effectiveness of Treatments

Reevaluating Products: Periodically reassess the products and treatments you're using to determine whether they are still effective. Hair may develop different needs over time, and what worked in the past may no longer be suitable.

Consulting a Specialist: If you're dealing with ongoing hair issues such as significant hair loss, scalp irritation, or changes in texture, consult a dermatologist or trichologist. These specialists can help diagnose underlying conditions and recommend targeted treatments.

10.6 Maintaining Healthy Lifestyle Habits

Long-term hair health is closely tied to overall health and wellness. Lifestyle habits like diet, exercise, yoga, meditation and stress management play a critical role in supporting hair growth and preventing damage.

10.6.1 Nutrition and Hydration

Balanced Diet: A diet rich in vitamins, minerals, and proteins is essential for healthy hair. Incorporate nutrient-dense foods like carrots, tomatoes, almonds, walnuts, fruits, leafy greens, soybeans, sprouts, pulses, eggs, and whole grains into your diet. Having higher life force energy in your diet is crucial aspect which we have discussed in previous chapters. Cyclical nutritional Supplements also support hair health, especially if your diet is not adequate.

Staying Hydrated: Hydration is key to maintaining a healthy scalp and strong hair. Ensure you drink at least 8 glasses of water per day, and increase your intake if you're active or live in a hot climate.

10.6.2 Stress Management

Mind-Body Connection: As discussed in Chapter 6, stress can negatively affect hair health by triggering hair loss conditions like Telogen effluvium or exacerbating existing scalp issues. Incorporating stress-reducing practices like yoga, meditation, or mindfulness into your routine can increasing the coping ability and help maintain hormonal balance and promote hair growth.

Adequate Sleep: Quality sleep is essential for tissue repair and hair growth. Aim for 6-8 hours of sleep each night to support the body's natural repair processes, including the regeneration of hair follicles. Early to bed and early to rise, makes a man healthy and wise.

10.7 Addressing New Challenges: Hair Loss Prevention and Treatment

Even with a consistent routine, new challenges such as hormonal changes, aging, or stress may impact your hair health. Having a plan in place for addressing these challenges will help you maintain long-term hair vitality.

10.7.1 Preventing Hair Loss

Early Intervention: If you notice early signs of hair thinning or excessive shedding, it's important to act quickly. Treatments like minoxidil or iPRF therapy in conjunction with Cyclical Nutritional therapy can be more effective when started early in the hair loss process with assistance of a dermatologist.

Regular Scalp Care: Keeping the scalp healthy is key to preventing hair loss. Regular exfoliation, scalp massage, and the use of growth-stimulating treatments like minoxidil can help keep hair follicles functioning properly.

10.7.2 Adjusting Treatments Over Time

Switching Products: As hair ages, it may require more hydration, less protein, or a gentler approach. Don't be afraid to switch products if your hair care routine is no longer meeting your needs. For instance, those transitioning into menopause may benefit from more moisturizing or scalp-balancing products.

Evaluating New Treatments: Stay informed about emerging treatments in hair care and hair loss prevention. New technologies like exosome therapy, stem cell therapy, or advanced supplements may become part of your long-term hair care strategy as they become available and clinically validated.

10.8 Real-Life Success Stories and Practical Tips

Understanding how others have successfully maintained their hair health over time can provide motivation and insights for your own journey. This section highlights real-life success stories of individuals who have effectively adapted their hair care routines to sustain long-term hair health.

10.8.1 Case Study: Maintaining Hair Health After Pregnancy

The Challenge: A 35-year-old woman experienced postpartum hair shedding after her second pregnancy. She noticed significant thinning around her temples and was concerned about the long-term effects of hormonal changes on her hair.

The Solution: She consulted me at my clinic and was recommended minoxidil and a cyclical nutritional hair supplement. Additionally, she incorporated regular scalp massages and adjusted her diet to include more iron-rich foods. After six months of consistent care, her hair began to regrow, and the shedding slowed significantly.

Results: By maintaining her adjusted hair care routine and addressing her nutritional needs, she successfully restored her hair to its pre-pregnancy thickness.

10.8.2 Practical Tips for Long-Term Success

Be Adaptable: Your hair care routine should evolve with your hair's needs. Stay flexible and willing to adjust products, treatments, and practices as your hair changes over time.

Stay Patient: Hair growth is a slow process, so it's important to be patient and consistent with your routine. Significant results may take several months, but persistence will pay off in the long run.

Focus on Overall Health: Healthy hair is a reflection of overall well-being. Prioritize good nutrition, hydration, optimize coping ability to stress management, and adequate quality sleep to support long-term hair health.

Conclusion

Maintaining long-term hair health requires a consistent, personalized approach that adapts to changes in your hair and lifestyle. By taking preventive measures, staying consistent with your hair care routine, and addressing challenges like aging, stress, or health conditions, you can preserve the vitality of your hair over time. Remember, hair care is a journey that involves not only the right products and treatments but also attention to overall health and well-being. In the final chapter, we will explore the psychological impact of hair health and offer insights on maintaining confidence and self-esteem throughout your hair care journey.

CHAPTER ELEVEN

Psychological Impact of Hair Health and Building Confidence

Hair plays a significant role in how we perceive ourselves and how others see us. Throughout history, hair has been tied to cultural identity, beauty standards, and personal expression. As such, changes in hair health - whether due to thinning, hair loss, or other concerns - can have profound psychological effects. This chapter explores the emotional and psychological impact of hair health, the relationship between hair and self-esteem, and strategies for maintaining confidence throughout your hair care journey, regardless of its challenges.

11.1 The Emotional Connection to Hair

Hair is deeply intertwined with identity and self-expression. For many, it represents a sense of beauty, youth, and vitality. When hair health declines, it can lead to feelings of anxiety, frustration, and even depression.

11.1.1 Hair and Identity

Cultural and Social Significance: Across various cultures, hair is more than just a physical feature - it symbolizes status, identity, and even spiritual beliefs. In many societies, thick, healthy hair is associated with vitality and youth, while hair loss or thinning may be perceived as a sign of aging or illness.

Personal Expression: Hair is also a medium of self-expression. Hairstyles, color, and texture choices allow individuals to reflect their personalities, beliefs, or changes in life circumstances. For some, changing their hairstyle marks major life transitions, such as a new career, relationship, or personal transformation.

11.1.2 The Emotional Toll of Hair Loss

Hair Loss and Self-Esteem: Hair loss, whether gradual or sudden, can have a significant impact on self-esteem. Many people experiencing hair loss feel a loss of control over their appearance, which can lead to feelings of helplessness or reduced confidence.

Social Anxiety and Avoidance: Some individuals with noticeable hair thinning or bald spots may become self-conscious in social situations. This can lead to avoidance behaviors, such as wearing hats or wigs, or even withdrawing from social interactions altogether. The emotional burden of hair loss can lead to anxiety and a preoccupation with appearance, affecting overall mental health.

Psychological Impact of Hair Thinning: Even mild thinning can affect one's perception of themselves. The process of losing hair can feel like losing part of one's identity, leading to emotional distress, especially in a society where thick, full hair is often idealized.

11.2 Understanding the Psychological Effects of Hair Loss

The psychological impact of hair loss extends beyond self-esteem, touching various aspects of mental health. For many individuals, hair loss can trigger deeper emotional responses that require support and coping mechanisms.

11.2.1 Depression and Hair Loss

Emotional Cycle of Hair Loss: Hair loss can lead to depression, particularly when it affects one's sense of identity and self-worth. The emotional cycle often begins with shock or denial, followed by frustration, anger, or sadness as the hair loss progresses. Without proper coping strategies, these feelings can lead to a deeper sense of hopelessness and disconnect with your inner self-consciousness.

Clinical Depression: In severe cases, individuals experiencing hair loss may develop clinical depression, characterized by persistent feelings of sadness, worthlessness, or loss of interest in previously enjoyable activities. Depression can also exacerbate hair loss by affecting overall health, nutrition, and self-care practices. I have seen many young males losing their self-esteem due to sudden hair loss and baldness. Their performance in office deteriorates which leads to isolation.

11.2.2 Anxiety and Obsessive Thoughts

Hair Loss Anxiety: The uncertainty surrounding hair loss - whether it will continue, worsen, or stop can cause anxiety. This anxiety may manifest in the form of obsessive thoughts about hair appearance, constant checking in mirrors, or frequent use of hair products and treatments. The patient starts searching and reading about hair loss on internet and gets even more confused. Patient later lands up trying heavily marketed products sold online. These products do not work most of the times which again leads to anxiety.

Body Dysmorphic Disorder (BDD): In some cases, hair loss can trigger or exacerbate Body Dysmorphic Disorder, a mental health condition where individuals become preoccupied with perceived flaws in their appearance. BDD sufferers may spend excessive time trying to cover up their hair loss or avoid mirrors and social interactions altogether.

11.2.3 The Impact on Relationships and Social Life

Social Withdrawal: People experiencing hair loss may withdraw from social situations due to embarrassment or fear of judgment. This can strain relationships with family, friends, and partners, leading to feelings of isolation.

Effects on Intimacy: Hair loss can affect intimate relationships, especially if one partner feels less attractive or confident. This is more common in females. Open communication about the emotional impact of hair loss is essential for maintaining a healthy relationship dynamic.

11.3 Coping with the Emotional Effects of Hair Loss

Coping with hair loss involves addressing both the physical and emotional aspects of the condition. Building resilience and finding healthy ways to manage the emotional effects of hair loss can improve overall well-being.

11.3.1 Building Emotional Resilience

Acceptance: One of the first steps in coping with hair loss is learning to accept the changes in your appearance. While this process takes time, acceptance can reduce feelings of helplessness and allow you to focus on proactive solutions, such as treatments or new hairstyles.

Mindfulness and Meditation: Practicing mindfulness can help reduce the emotional stress of hair loss. Mindfulness techniques, such as deep breathing and meditation, encourage a focus on the present moment, reducing anxiety about future hair loss or past changes in appearance. Meditation helps to elevate the coping ability which then reduces stress.

Positive Affirmations : Incorporating positive affirmations into your daily routine can help build confidence and improve self-esteem. Simple phrases like “I am more than my appearance” or “I am confident and capable” can shift your mindset from focusing on physical changes to embracing inner strength. You can take help of many positive affirmation’s app available. There are wonderful positive affirmations on Brahmakumaris organization website portals, which can be quite helpful.

11.3.2 Seeking Support

Therapy and Counseling: For those experiencing significant emotional distress, seeking therapy or counseling can provide valuable support. Cognitive-behavioral therapy (CBT), in particular, can help individuals reframe negative thoughts about their hair loss and build coping strategies.

Support Groups: Joining a hair loss support group, either in person or online, can help individuals connect with others going through similar experiences. Sharing stories, tips, and emotional struggles can reduce feelings of isolation and provide encouragement.

Talking to Loved Ones: Open communication with friends and family is essential. Sharing your feelings about hair loss with those closest to you can help them understand your emotional experience, provide support, and reduce misunderstandings.

11.4 Redefining Beauty and Self-Worth

In a society where thick, luscious hair is often considered a standard of beauty, redefining what beauty and self-worth mean on a personal level is crucial for emotional well-being. Shifting your perspective from external appearance to internal qualities can help you embrace a healthier mindset.

11.4.1 Challenging Beauty Standards

Questioning Societal Norms: It's important to recognize that societal beauty standards are often unrealistic and narrow. These standards can put unnecessary pressure on individuals to conform, leading to feelings of inadequacy when changes, such as hair loss, occur. By questioning these norms and recognizing that beauty comes in many forms, you can begin to detach your self-worth from physical appearance.

Body Positivity and Self-Acceptance: Embracing body positivity encourages a healthier relationship with your body and appearance. Accepting that hair changes are a natural part of life and do not define your worth is a key component of building confidence. Celebrating all body types, hair textures, and stages of life can help normalize hair loss and reduce the stigma around it.

11.4.2 Focusing on Inner Qualities

Shifting the Focus to Inner Strengths: Focusing on your inner qualities - such as kindness, resilience, and creativity - rather than external appearance can help boost self-esteem. Take time to acknowledge your accomplishments and personal strengths that have nothing to do with how you look.

Developing New Interests: Hair loss can be an opportunity to shift focus from appearance to other aspects of life. Developing new hobbies, skills, or interests can help build confidence and give a sense of purpose beyond physical appearance.

11.5 Building Confidence Through Hair Care and Styling

For those experiencing hair thinning or loss, hair care and styling can still be powerful tools for building confidence. Whether through choosing flattering styles, experimenting with wigs or hairpieces, or using treatments to enhance growth, finding a hair routine that works for you can make a significant difference in how you feel about your appearance.

11.5.1 Choosing the Right Hairstyles

Flattering Styles for Thinning Hair: There are many haircuts and styles designed to make thinning hair look fuller. For example, layered cuts add volume, while shorter styles can make hair appear thicker. Working with a professional stylist to find a look that flatters your hair type and face shape can boost confidence.

Protective Styles: Protective styles, such as braids, twists, or buns, are excellent for preventing damage and breakage. These styles are particularly useful for individuals with textured hair who want to minimize manipulation and support healthy hair growth.

11.5.2 Wigs, Hairpieces, and Extensions

Exploring Hair Alternatives: Wigs, hairpieces, and extensions offer a versatile solution for those experiencing significant hair loss or thinning. With advances in technology, these products look more natural than ever and provide individuals with the option to change their look based on their mood or occasion.

Choosing a Wig or Hairpiece: When selecting a wig or hairpiece, consider your lifestyle, budget, and comfort level. Human hair wigs offer the most natural appearance and styling flexibility but are more expensive than synthetic options. Synthetic wigs, on the other hand, require less maintenance and hold their shape longer.

Embracing Hair Alternatives: While wigs and hairpieces are often used to conceal hair loss, many individuals find empowerment in the versatility they offer. Viewing these options as a form of self-expression, rather than a necessity, can change the way you feel about wearing them.

11.5.3 Hair Growth Treatments for Confidence

Commitment to Treatment Plans: For individuals looking to regain hair, adhering to a treatment plan with products like minoxidil, iPRF therapy or low-level laser therapy (LLLT) can provide a sense of control and empowerment. These treatments can help slow hair loss, promote hair thickness, and improve hair density, leading to greater confidence.

Setting Realistic Expectations: While some hair growth treatments can produce significant results, it's essential to set realistic expectations. Improvements in hair density or thickness may take several months to become noticeable, and some treatments may need to be continued long-term to maintain results.

11.6 Embracing Hair Changes with Confidence

For some, embracing hair loss rather than attempting to conceal or reverse it can lead to a sense of empowerment and freedom. Many individuals find confidence in accepting their natural hair changes, whether that means going completely bald or embracing graying or thinning hair.

11.6.1 Shaving the Head

The Bold Step of Shaving: For individuals who prefer not to deal with thinning hair, shaving the head can be an empowering choice. Many men and women who shave their heads report feeling liberated from societal beauty standards and gaining a renewed sense of confidence.

Maintaining a Shaved Look: A well-maintained shaved head requires regular upkeep. Keeping the scalp moisturized and protected from the sun with SPF products is essential. Some individuals choose to incorporate scalp tattoos (Scalp Micropigmentation) to create the appearance of hair follicles, adding definition to a shaved head.

11.6.2 Embracing Natural Hair Changes

Accepting Gray Hair: Many people choose to embrace their natural gray hair rather than dyeing it. Gray hair can be striking and sophisticated, and there is a growing movement toward celebrating natural aging processes. Proper care, including moisturizing and conditioning products, can keep gray hair healthy and vibrant.

Celebrating Individuality: Accepting your hair as it is - whether it's thinning, graying, or changing in texture, can be a powerful way to embrace individuality. By viewing hair changes as a natural part of life, you can cultivate self-acceptance and confidence.

11.7 Real-Life Applications: Stories of Confidence and Resilience

Hearing the stories of individuals who have navigated the emotional challenges of hair loss can offer inspiration and practical insights. Here are a few real-life examples of people who found ways to build confidence through their hair journeys.

11.7.1 Case Study: Reclaiming Confidence After Hair Loss

The Challenge: A 45-year-old woman began experiencing hair thinning due to hormonal changes during menopause. Initially devastated by the changes in her hair, she felt self-conscious in social settings and struggled with her self-image.

The Solution: After consultation, she started using minoxidil and incorporated scalp massages into her routine. She also embraced a shorter, layered haircut that gave the appearance of fuller hair. In addition to these practical steps, she began practicing mindfulness meditation to manage stress and improve her self-esteem.

Results: Within six months, she noticed improvements in both her hair and her confidence. By focusing on what she could control and learning to accept the natural aging process, she regained her sense of self-worth and began to feel more comfortable in social situations.

11.7.2 Case Study: Embracing Baldness with Confidence

The Challenge: A 30-year-old man with early-onset male pattern baldness found himself increasingly preoccupied with covering up his thinning hair. He spent significant time and money on treatments, wigs, and hairpieces but felt frustrated with the lack of consistent results.

The Solution: After years of struggling, he decided to shave his head completely. Though initially hesitant, he quickly found that the shaved look suited his lifestyle and made him feel more in control of his appearance. He embraced the new look by incorporating stylish accessories like hats and sunglasses to complement his shaved head.

Results: Shaving his head gave him a renewed sense of confidence. He no longer felt burdened by hiding his hair loss and was able to focus on other aspects of his life and personal development. He found that accepting his baldness allowed him to regain confidence in social and professional settings.

Conclusion

Hair health is about more than physical appearance - it's tied to our emotional well-being, confidence, and sense of identity. For many, changes in hair health, such as thinning or loss, can be deeply distressing. However, by embracing positive coping strategies, challenging societal beauty standards, and focusing on inner strengths, it's possible to maintain confidence throughout the hair care journey.

Whether through treatments, hairstyles, or self-acceptance, finding the approach that works best for you is key to building a sense of empowerment. Finally, we will discuss how to maintain a balanced, holistic approach to hair care and well-being, drawing on the lessons learned throughout this book to support both hair health and overall wellness in the final conclusion of this book.

Conclusion The Journey To Healthy Hair

The journey to healthy hair is not merely a physical process but a profound path of self-discovery, patience, consciousness and balance. Throughout this book, we've explored the interconnectedness of mind, body, meditation and spirit in achieving true hair wellness. From understanding the science of hair growth and incorporating modern treatments to embracing ancient practices like yoga and meditation, gut microbiome and life force energy of food, the pursuit of healthy hair is a holistic endeavor.

Recap of Key Concepts

At the foundation of hair health is the understanding that our hair reflects our internal and external environment. We've learned that genetics, and more importantly epigenetics like hormonal balances, nutrition, lifestyle, pollution, infections, cosmetics usage, stress, and even the way we care for our scalp play pivotal roles in determining the quality and vitality of our hair. Hair loss, thinning, and breakage are not isolated events but are often signals from the body that something deeper needs attention.

We discussed **modern treatments**, such as minoxidil - topical and oral tablets, finasteride, dutasteride, melatonin, iPRF therapy, PRP therapy, and Cyclical Nutritional supplements, which offer scientifically-backed solutions to stimulate hair growth and prevent further loss. But these treatments work best when integrated with practices that nourish the whole being. These modern treatment will try to treat the hair loss, but won't be able to prevent the hair loss. So, it's very essential to integrate both preventive and therapeutic options for an overall holistic approach for hair health.

The **holistic path to hair wellness** emphasized that hair health begins long before any product touches the scalp. It starts with what we feed our bodies - both physically and mentally. A nutrient-rich diet with high life force energy which maintains a good gut microbiome, coupled with stress-reduction practices like Raj Yoga meditation, allows the body to heal from within. **The power of yoga**, daily walks, and mindfulness encourages improved circulation to the scalp, reduced cortisol levels, and deeper inner peace, all of which foster stronger hair follicles and healthier growth.

Finally, **scalp care** emerged as a central focus - a healthy scalp with healthy scalp microbiome being the fertile ground from which vibrant hair can grow. Proper cleansing, exfoliation, and moisturizing, combined with regular scalp massages, were shown to not only support hair growth but to transform hair care from a routine into a nourishing ritual of self-care.

Embrace the Journey, Not Just the Destination

Healthy hair is not an instant transformation, but a **journey** that demands patience, consistency, and self-compassion. Often, we become fixated on results waiting for our hair to grow thicker, longer, or fuller, but the true transformation happens when we shift our mindset. We need to understand that healthy epigenetic lifestyle leads to healthy hair. Poor epigenetic lifestyle leads to hair loss and hair thinning. Many times, we just focus on outcome related behavioral changes in our life like treating the hair loss with modern medications itself. However, we need to understand that we have to go deeper and bring personality related behavioral changes of better epigenetic lifestyle like yoga, meditation, morning walk, healthy balanced diet with higher life force energy to bring long lasting consistent results. When we embrace the journey itself, we begin to honor our bodies and the natural rhythms of life.

Along the way, setbacks may occur. There will be moments of frustration when progress seems slow or when hair loss feels overwhelming. But these moments offer an opportunity to reflect on the broader picture. Hair health is intimately tied to how we treat our bodies, how we built our coping abilities, how we manage stress, and how we care for our mental and emotional well-being. Each step we take towards better health, whether through nutrition, meditation, yoga or simply taking time to rest is a step toward healthier hair, but more importantly, a step toward a healthier, more balanced life.

Final Encouragement: A Profound Shift

This journey is about more than hair, it's about discovering a **deeper connection to yourself**. Your hair becomes a reflection of your overall vitality, a testament to how well you care for the totality of your being. As you embrace this holistic path, let go of the obsession with immediate results and trust the process.

There's a profound transformation that happens when you realize that your **worth is not defined by your appearance**. The changes you make today like getting up early, performing morning ritual of meditation, yoga and walk, choosing to eat better, move your body, or take moments of stillness are all acts of love toward yourself. They will, in time, manifest in stronger, healthier hair, but more importantly, they will lead to a greater sense of inner peace and well-being.

Remember, **the destination is not just a head of healthy hair**, but a life in which you honor your body, mind, and spirit. Each day you choose to care for yourself, you are nourishing not only your hair but also your deepest self. And that, in itself, is a victory.

As you walk this path, know that the journey will shape you in ways far beyond what you see in the mirror. It's an opportunity to embrace patience, resilience, and self-love qualities that will enrich every area of your life. Your hair is but one expression of the balance and harmony you create within.

Embrace this journey, not as a task to be completed, but as an evolving process of self-care and empowerment. **You are more than your hair, and the journey to wellness is yours to own and celebrate.**

Appendix A: Glossary Of Key Terms

This appendix provides definitions and explanations of key terms used throughout the book, offering clarity on technical and medical concepts related to hair health, treatments, and holistic wellness.

1. Anagen Phase

The active growth phase of the hair cycle, during which hair follicles are producing new hair. This phase can last anywhere from 2 to 7 years, depending on genetics and other factors. Healthy hair growth depends largely on the duration of the anagen phase.

2. Androgenetic Alopecia

A common form of hair loss, also known as male or female pattern baldness. This condition is typically caused by genetics and hormones, particularly dihydrotestosterone (DHT), which leads to the miniaturization of hair follicles and gradual hair thinning.

3. Body Dysmorphic Disorder (BDD)

A mental health condition where individuals become obsessively concerned with perceived flaws or defects in their appearance, which may not be noticeable to others. For some, hair thinning or hair loss can trigger or exacerbate BDD, leading to distress and anxiety.

4. Catagen Phase

The transitional phase of the hair cycle, during which hair growth slows and the follicle begins to shrink. This phase lasts for 2 to 3 weeks and signals the end of the active growth phase.

5. Corticosteroids

A class of anti-inflammatory medications often used to treat scalp conditions like psoriasis and eczema. Corticosteroids can reduce inflammation, soothe itching, and manage flare-ups that can affect hair health.

6. Dihydrotestosterone (DHT)

A hormone derived from testosterone that plays a key role in Androgenetic alopecia. DHT binds to androgen receptors in hair follicles, causing them to shrink and eventually stop producing hair. Reducing DHT levels through medications like finasteride can help slow hair loss.

7. Exogen Phase

The phase of the hair cycle where hair is shed from the follicle. Typically, 50 to 100 hairs are shed daily as part of the natural hair cycle, though excessive shedding may indicate telogen effluvium or other hair loss conditions.

8. Finasteride

An oral medication that reduces the conversion of testosterone to DHT, often prescribed to treat male pattern baldness. Finasteride helps slow the progression of hair loss and promotes hair regrowth by inhibiting the hormone that contributes to follicle shrinkage.

9. Follicular Unit Extraction (FUE)

A hair transplant technique where individual hair follicles are harvested from the donor area (usually the back of the scalp) and transplanted to areas with thinning or baldness. FUE leaves minimal scarring compared to the strip method (FUT).

10. Follicular Unit Transplantation (FUT)

A hair transplant method that involves removing a strip of scalp from the donor area to extract hair follicles for transplantation. While FUT can transplant a large number of follicles, it may leave a linear scar at the donor site.

11. Hair Follicle

A small, tubular structure in the skin from which hair grows. Each follicle undergoes a cycle of growth, rest, and shedding, and is nourished by blood vessels that supply oxygen and nutrients to promote hair growth.

12. Ketoconazole

An antifungal agent commonly used in medicated shampoos to treat dandruff and seborrheic dermatitis. Ketoconazole helps control the overgrowth of yeast on the scalp, reducing flaking and irritation.

13. Low-Level Laser Therapy (LLLT)

A non-invasive treatment for hair loss that uses red or near-infrared light to stimulate hair follicles and promote hair growth. LLLT devices, such as laser combs and helmets, are designed for at-home use and are particularly effective for Androgenetic alopecia.

14. Minoxidil

A topical medication approved by the FDA for treating hair loss. Minoxidil stimulates hair follicles and prolongs the anagen phase of the hair cycle, promoting regrowth. It is available in both 2% and 5% formulations and is used by both men and women.

15. Platelet-Rich Plasma (PRP) Therapy

A treatment that involves injecting platelet-rich plasma (derived from the patient's own blood) into the scalp to stimulate hair growth. PRP contains growth factors that promote healing and hair follicle regeneration, and it is often used to treat Androgenetic alopecia and other forms of hair loss.

16. Raj Yoga

A form of yoga that focuses on mental and spiritual discipline through meditation and mindfulness. Raj Yoga aims to bring balance to the mind and body, helping reduce stress, which is a known contributor to hair loss. Practicing Raj Yoga can promote inner peace and support overall well-being, including hair health.

17. Seborrheic Dermatitis

A common skin condition that affects the scalp, causing flaking, redness, and irritation. It is often linked to an overgrowth of yeast on the scalp and is commonly treated with medicated shampoos containing ketoconazole or zinc pyrithione.

18. Scalp Micropigmentation (SMP)

A non-surgical cosmetic procedure that involves tattooing tiny dots on the scalp to create the appearance of hair follicles. SMP can mimic the look of closely-shaven hair or add density to areas of thinning, providing a fuller appearance.

19. Telogen Phase

The resting phase of the hair cycle, during which hair growth ceases and the follicle rests before the hair is eventually shed. Telogen effluvium occurs when an unusually large number of hairs enter this phase simultaneously, leading to excessive shedding.

20. Telogen Effluvium

A form of temporary hair loss that occurs when stress, illness, hormonal changes, or other factors cause a large number of hairs to enter the resting (telogen) phase. Telogen effluvium typically resolves on its own once the underlying cause is addressed.

21. Traction Alopecia

A form of hair loss caused by prolonged tension on the hair follicles, often due to tight hairstyles like braids, ponytails, or extensions. Traction alopecia can lead to permanent hair loss if not addressed early by loosening hairstyles and reducing strain on the scalp.

22. Trichologist

A specialist in the science of hair and scalp health. Trichologists are trained to diagnose and treat a wide range of hair and scalp conditions, including hair loss, dandruff, and scalp disorders.

23. Vitamin D Deficiency

A deficiency in vitamin D, which plays a role in hair follicle cycling and overall scalp health. Low levels of vitamin D have been linked to conditions like alopecia areata and can contribute to hair thinning and loss. Ensuring adequate vitamin D levels through sun exposure, diet, or supplements can support healthy hair growth.

24. Zinc Pyrithione

An antifungal and antibacterial agent commonly used in dandruff shampoos to control flaking, itching, and irritation on the scalp. Zinc pyrithione helps reduce the overgrowth of yeast and bacteria that contribute to scalp conditions like seborrheic dermatitis.

This glossary serves as a reference for the key terms and concepts discussed throughout the book. Understanding these terms will help you make informed decisions on your hair health journey and better navigate conversations with healthcare providers, hair specialists, and wellness practitioners.

Appendix B: Cited Studies, Resources For Further Reading

This appendix provides a list of scientific studies, books, and articles cited throughout the book. These resources offer deeper insights into hair health, modern treatments, and holistic wellness approaches. It also includes recommended books and articles for further reading on hair care, nutrition, and stress management.

1. Scientific Studies and Research Articles

a. Hair Growth and Hair Loss Treatments

Rogers, N. E., & Avram, M. R. (2008).*Medical treatments for male and female pattern hair loss.* Journal of the American Academy of Dermatology, 59(4), 547-566.

This comprehensive review covers FDA-approved treatments like minoxidil and finasteride, discussing their efficacy and mechanisms of action in treating androgenetic alopecia.

Yoo, H. G., Kim, J. S., Lee, S. R., & Pyo, S. W. (2010).*The effects of minoxidil on hair follicular cells.*International Journal of Dermatology, 49(12), 1371-1375.
A study that examines the molecular effects of minoxidil on hair follicle cells, showing how it prolongs the anagen phase and promotes hair regrowth.

Gupta, A. K., & Carviel, J. L. (2017).*Platelet-rich plasma (PRP) for androgenetic alopecia: A review of the evidence.* Journal of Cosmetic Dermatology, 16(4), 567-572.
This article evaluates the effectiveness of PRP therapy in promoting hair growth, summarizing clinical findings on its use for androgenetic alopecia.

Suchonwanit, P., Thammarucha, S., & Leerunyakul, K. (2019).*Minoxidil and its use in hair disorders: A review.* Drug Design, Development, and Therapy, 13, 2777-2786.

A detailed review of minoxidil's application in hair disorders, including its efficacy in male and female pattern hair loss.

b. Holistic and Nutritional Approaches to Hair Health:

Chacon, J. I., Suneja, T., & Bergfeld, W. F. (2020).*The role of nutrition in hair loss: A review.* Dermatologic Therapy, 33(6), e14041.
This article reviews the impact of various nutritional deficiencies, including iron, zinc, and biotin, on hair loss and provides recommendations for dietary supplementation.

Arck, P. C., Handjiski, B., Hagen, E., & Peters, E. M. (2001).*Stress inhibits hair growth in mice by induction of premature catagen development and TGF-beta1 expression.* FASEB Journal, 15(13), 2536-2538.
A study exploring how stress triggers hair loss by altering the hair cycle, providing a biological basis for the relationship between stress and hair thinning.

Bakry, O. A., Basha, M. A., & Eid, H. H. (2017).*The efficacy of yoga and meditation in treating telogen effluvium.* Journal of Clinical and Diagnostic Research, 11(7), WC01-WC03.
A clinical study examining how yoga and meditation can reduce telogen effluvium caused by chronic stress and hormonal imbalances.

c. Scalp Health and Care:

Borda, L. J., & Wikramanayake, T. C. (2015).*Seborrheic dermatitis and dandruff: A comprehensive review.*Journal of Clinical and Investigative Dermatology, 3(2), 1-10.
A detailed review of scalp conditions like seborrheic dermatitis and dandruff, discussing treatment options including medicated shampoos and anti-inflammatory agents.

Berger, R. S., & Fu, J. L. (2018).*The benefits of scalp massage for hair growth stimulation.* International Journal of Trichology, 10(4), 170-178.

Research on the physiological effects of scalp massage in improving blood circulation to hair follicles, supporting the idea that regular scalp stimulation can enhance hair growth.

2. Recommended Books

a. Hair Care and Science:

"The Science of Black Hair: A Comprehensive Guide to Textured Hair Care" by Audrey Davis-Sivasothy.
This book provides an in-depth exploration of textured hair care, with a strong focus on the science of hair health, maintenance, and the unique challenges faced by those with textured hair.

"Healthy Hair: What Science Can Teach You About Hair Care" by R. Randall Wickett.
A detailed look at the science of hair structure, growth, and damage, with insights into choosing the right products and treatments based on scientific evidence.

"The Hair Loss Cure: A Self-Help Guide" by David H. Kingsley.
Written by a certified trichologist, this book offers practical advice for diagnosing and treating hair loss through both traditional and holistic methods.

b. Holistic Health and Wellness:

"The Ayurvedic Guide to Diet and Weight Loss: The Sattva Program" by Kristen Schneider.
This book explains Ayurvedic principles of health, including how diet and lifestyle can affect not only weight but also hair health. It provides guidance on how to balance doshas to improve overall wellness, including hair vitality.

"Yoga for Hair Growth: The Ultimate Guide" by Angela Stevens.
A practical guide to using yoga poses and breathing techniques to improve blood flow to the scalp, reduce stress, and support hair growth naturally.

"The Self-Care Solution: A Year of Becoming Happier, Healthier, and Fitter—One Month at a Time" by Jennifer Ashton, M.D.
This book promotes the idea of holistic self-care, offering tips on how small, consistent changes to diet, exercise, and mindfulness can improve both physical and emotional well-being, which ultimately impacts hair health.

3. Articles and Online Resources

a. Dermatologists and Trichologists:

Consult with certified dermatologists and trichologists to get expert guidance on diagnosing and treating hair loss conditions. Hair specialists can offer personalized treatment plans based on your specific needs, including prescription medications, topical treatments, and therapies like PRP.
American Academy of Dermatology (AAD):www.aad.org
International Society of Hair Restoration Surgery (ISHRS):www.ishrs.org

b. Research on Hair Loss and Treatments:

Access peer-reviewed studies and up-to-date research on hair loss, the effectiveness of treatments like minoxidil, finasteride, and PRP, and new advancements in the field.
PubMed:www.pubmed.ncbi.nlm.nih.gov
Journal of Cosmetic Dermatology:www.onlinelibrary.wiley.com

c. Articles on Hair Loss Treatments:

"Hair Loss Treatments: Options for Men and Women" – Mayo Clinic.

https://www.mayoclinic.org
This article provides an overview of hair loss causes and the most effective medical and surgical treatments available today.
"How Stress Affects Your Hair Health" – Harvard Health Publishing.
https://www.health.harvard.edu
Discusses the direct link between chronic stress and hair loss, including how stress-related conditions like telogen effluvium develop.

d. Websites for Nutritional and Holistic Health:

"The Nutrition Source – Healthy Eating Plate & Guidelines" – Harvard T.H. Chan School of Public Health.
https://www.hsph.harvard.edu/nutritionsource
Provides evidence-based recommendations for a balanced diet, including the nutrients necessary for maintaining healthy hair.

"Yoga with Adriene" – Free Online Yoga Classes for Stress Relief.
https://www.youtube.com/user/yogawithadriene
A popular YouTube channel offering free yoga classes, including those designed to reduce stress, improve circulation, and support overall well-being.

Community and Support Networks:
"Hair Loss Talk – Online Forum and Resources for Hair Loss Support"
https://www.hairlosstalk.com
A robust online forum where individuals share their experiences with hair loss treatments, provide emotional support, and discuss new therapies.
"Headspace – Meditation and Mindfulness App"
https://www.headspace.com
This app offers guided meditation practices that help manage stress and anxiety, both of which play a key role in hair health.

Final Note

The references and resources listed here offer a blend of scientific research, practical advice, and holistic approaches to hair health. Whether you're looking for deeper insights into medical treatments or exploring natural ways to improve your hair and well-being, these materials will support your journey to stronger, healthier hair and overall wellness.

Appendix C: Frequently Asked Questions (faq)

This appendix addresses common questions about hair health, treatments, and holistic practices. The goal is to provide clarity on key concepts and help readers better understand how to care for their hair effectively.

1. Hair Growth and Hair Loss

Q: How long does it take to see results from hair growth treatments like minoxidil or iPRF therapy?

A: Hair growth treatments generally take time to show results, as hair follows a slow growth cycle. For **minoxidil**, it can take **3-6 months** of consistent use before noticeable improvements appear. Results may continue to improve with ongoing treatment. **iPRF therapy** often requires a series of treatments spaced over several months, and initial improvements are typically seen within **4-6 months**. Patience is key, as hair growth happens gradually.

Q: What's the difference between hair shedding and hair loss?

A: Hair shedding refers to the normal loss of 50-100 hairs per day as part of the hair's natural cycle. This is a normal process and does not typically result in noticeable thinning. **Hair loss**, on the other hand, occurs when there is a disruption in the hair cycle, leading to excessive shedding or an inability to regrow hair. Conditions like Androgenetic alopecia, Telogen effluvium, or autoimmune diseases such as Alopecia areata can cause hair loss.

Q: How do stress and anxiety affect hair health?

A: Chronic stress can significantly impact hair health. Stress increases levels of **cortisol**, a hormone that can disrupt the hair growth cycle and lead to **Telogen effluvium**, where hair enters the resting phase prematurely and falls out. Managing stress through techniques like yoga, meditation, or regular physical activity is essential for maintaining healthy hair.

2. Scalp Care

Q: How often should I wash my hair if I have an oily scalp?

A: If you have an **oily scalp**, washing your hair **2-3 times a week** is generally recommended to remove excess oil, dirt, and product buildup. Use a **clarifying shampoo** once a week to deep-clean the scalp without over-drying. However, washing every day with shampoo may strip your scalp of natural oils, leading to an overproduction of sebum, which worsens oiliness.

Q: What is scalp exfoliation, and why is it important?

A: Scalp exfoliation involves removing dead skin cells, excess oil, and product buildup from the scalp. It improves scalp health by clearing clogged follicles, promoting better circulation, and creating a healthy environment for hair growth. Exfoliating once a week with a gentle scrub or an exfoliating shampoo can help maintain a clean, balanced scalp.

Q: I have a sensitive scalp. How can I treat dandruff without irritating it further?

A: For a **sensitive scalp**, use a **sulfate-free, gentle anti-dandruff shampoo** that contains ingredients like **zinc pyrithione** or **salicylic acid**. These ingredients help reduce dandruff without being too harsh. Avoid over-scrubbing and always follow up with a mild conditioner to restore moisture. If the condition persists, consult a dermatologist for targeted treatments.

3. Holistic Hair Care

Q: How does yoga and meditation improve hair health?

A: Yoga and meditation improve hair health by promoting relaxation and reducing **stress**, which is a major contributor to hair loss. Practices like **Raj Yoga** help lower cortisol levels, balance hormones, and improve blood circulation to the scalp. Specific yoga poses, such as **Sirsasana (Headstand)** or **Sarvangasana (Shoulder Stand)**, boost scalp circulation, supporting healthier follicles and hair growth.

Q: Can diet really affect hair growth? What foods should I focus on?

A: Yes, diet plays a crucial role in hair growth. Hair is made primarily of protein (keratin), so consuming **protein-rich foods** like soybeans, sprouts, pulses and eggs are essential. Additionally, foods rich in **biotin**, **iron**, **omega-3 fatty acids**, and **zinc** (such as spinach, nuts, and seeds) help strengthen hair and prevent hair loss. Ensuring your body has the proper nutrients will directly impact the health and resilience of your hair.

Q: How often should I meditate or practice Raj Yoga to see benefits for my hair?

A: Consistency is key. **Practicing Raj Yoga or meditation for 15-30 minutes a day** early morning can help reduce stress levels, improve circulation, and promote overall well-being, which contributes to healthy hair. For best results, aim to incorporate Raj Yoga or meditation into your daily routine. The long-term benefits will support not only hair health but also your mental and physical wellness.

4. Hair Care Products and Treatments

Q: How do I choose the right shampoo for my hair type?

A: Choose a shampoo based on your **scalp type** and **hair needs**:

- For **oily scalps**, look for **clarifying or balancing shampoos** that control oil without stripping moisture.
- For **dry or sensitive scalps**, choose **sulfate-free, moisturizing shampoos** with ingredients like aloe vera or jojoba oil.
- If you have issues like **dandruff**, opt for a **medicated shampoo** with **zinc pyrithione** or **ketoconazole**. Always avoid harsh chemicals like sulfates and parabens, as they can cause dryness or irritation.

Q: Is it safe to use heat styling tools regularly?

A: Heat styling can damage the hair if done frequently without proper protection. If you use heat styling tools, always apply a **heat protectant**

spray before styling, keep the temperature on the lower side, and limit usage to a few times a week. Overuse of heat can lead to breakage, dryness, and split ends, so try to incorporate **heat-free styling** methods when possible.

Q: What are the side effects of using minoxidil?

A: Minoxidil is generally well-tolerated, but some users may experience side effects such as **scalp irritation, itching, or dryness**. In rare cases, increased hair shedding may occur in the early stages of use, which is typically temporary. It's important to follow the recommended dosage and consult a dermatologist if side effects persist or worsen.

5. Hair Growth and Maintenance

Q: How can I tell if a hair supplement is effective?

A: Hair supplements usually take a few months to show noticeable effects. To determine effectiveness, track your hair's thickness, texture, and growth over time. You can also take **before and after photos** to monitor changes. Additionally, consult an expert dermatologist to ensure the supplement is addressing any underlying nutritional deficiencies contributing to hair loss.

Q: Can I prevent hair loss completely?

A: While some forms of hair loss, such as **genetic or age-related hair loss**, cannot be entirely prevented, many causes of hair thinning can be mitigated. **Maintaining a healthy lifestyle**, managing stress by optimizing coping ability, eating a balanced diet with life force energy, and practicing gentle hair care can all help preserve hair health and slow the progression of hair loss. Early intervention with treatments like minoxidil or finasteride can also help reduce hair loss in those with Androgenetic alopecia with consult of an expert dermatologist.

Final Note

These FAQs are designed to clarify common concerns and provide practical advice for maintaining healthy hair. As your hair health journey progresses, remember to consult with professionals for personalized recommendations, stay patient with the process, and trust that holistic care can enhance not only your hair but your overall well-being.

www.ingramcontent.com/pod-product-compliance
Lightning Source LLC
LaVergne TN
LVHW021155160826
845679LV00024B/2130

* 9 7 9 8 8 9 5 5 6 6 9 5 4 *